The Bible

Its Origin, Transmission, and Translation

Curtis Byers

Guten Book Publishing

Nashville, Tennessee

The Bible:
Its Origin, Transmission, and Translation

Copyright © 2022 by Curtis Byers

Guten Book Publishing
Nashville, Tennessee
gutenbookpub@gmail.com

Latest updated 11/11/2023

ISBN 13 Number: 978-1-953850-05-8

Printed in the United States of America

Images on the Front Cover

Front Cover Image (Center): *Gutenberg Bible, Lenox Copy, New York Public Library, May 29, 2009. Flickr upload by NTC Wanderer (Kevin Eng). Wikimedia Commons.* Bought by James Lenox in 1847, it was the first copy to be acquired by a United States citizen.

Front Cover Image (Bottom Right): *Papyrus 52, Rylands Greek P 457 Recto, August 9, 2019, Rylands Imaging. Wikimedia Commons.* The earliest known fragment of any part of the New Testament; 8.9 x 5.8 cm; dated to AD 130; in the John Rylands University Library in Manchester. The front side (recto) shown contains a portion of John 18:31-33; the back side (verso) contains a portion of John 18:37-38.

Acknowledgment

It is a pleasure for me to acknowledge my indebtedness to the experts in this field of study. I am simply a layman with an interest in understanding the Bible. The writings of F.F. Bruce, Bruce Metzger, and Stanley Porter gave excellent guidance to my study and a framework on which I was able to build my understanding. The Bibliography gives a sense of the other scholars I have drawn from. My understanding is certainly incomplete, and may even be flawed, but I have tried to correctly convey what is known in this field.

I am deeply indebted to my publisher and friend, Jeremy Sweets with Guten Book Publishing, for encouraging me to make this study available.

My greatest debt is to God the Father and His Son Christ Jesus. Without the strength they provide, I could accomplish nothing.

Table of Contents

Introduction

The Bible remains the perennial best-selling book and has been at least partially translated into about 2,400 contemporary languages that represent about 90% of the world's population. Even with such popularity, the history of the Bible is obscure to the vast majority of its readers. For most people who identify as "Christian", the Bible is the written record of God's reveled will. That is, it is divine in its origin. But it was placed in the hands of men who have collected, copied and translated it. From the scribes who devoted their lives to the copying of Scripture to those, like William Tyndale, who sacrificed their lives to ensure that the common person could read the Bible in their native tongue, the Bible has been passed down and preserved for our use today. It is that story that will be told in this study.

For those who acknowledged the divine origin of the Bible, the fundamental question is whether our English Bible is a faithful rendition of the original writings. Sir Frederic Kenyon clearly states the importance of this question.

"The foundation of all study of the Bible, with which the reader must acquaint himself if his study is to be securely based, is the knowledge of its history as a book. The English reader of the Bible knows that he is reading a translation of books written in other languages many centuries ago. If he wishes to assure himself of the claim which these books have on his consideration, he must know when and under what circumstances they were written, and how they have been handed down through the ages. He needs to be satisfied that he has the text of them substantially in a correct form." [Frederic Kenyon, *Our Bible and the Ancient Manuscripts*, 19]

It is this process of transmitting the Bible that must be understood if we are to have assurance that our English Bible is trustworthy. Of course, there is not just one English Bible; numerous English translations are available. Thus, another emphasis of this study is to appreciate the issues that impact the quality of an English translation so that we can wisely select and use translations.

Establishing the trustworthiness of our Bibles is not simply an intellectual pursuit. It is the starting point for all who truly want to know the God who revealed himself to us in the Bible.

All praise and glory to the God who is not silent.

All comments are welcomed. You can email me at curtis.d.byers@gmail.com.

Note: All Scripture quotations are from the ESV, unless noted otherwise.

The Bible: A Historical Overview

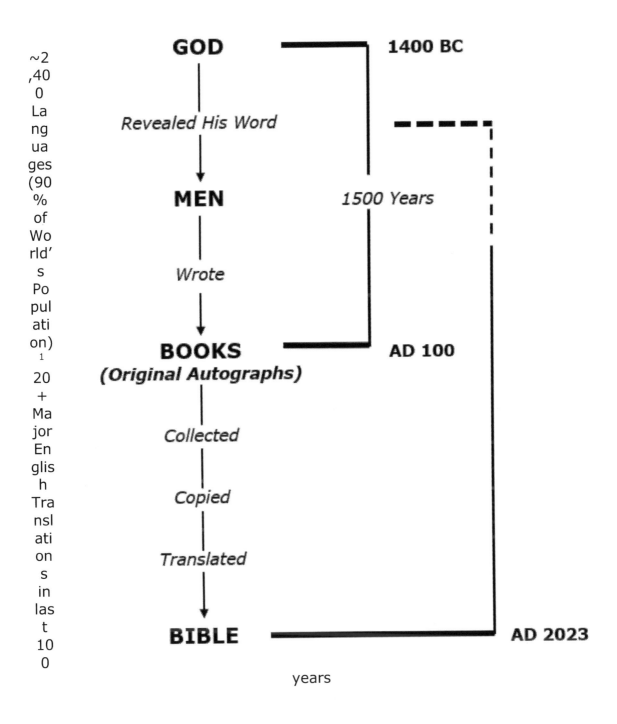

~2,400 Languages (90% of World's Population)[1]

20+ Major English Translations in last 100

years

[1] As of September, 2023, the Wycliffe Global Alliance reports that the entire Bible had been translated into 736 languages, the New Testament into 1,658 languages representing approximately 90% of the world population. [https://www.wycliffe.net/resources/statistics/]

Pronunciation Guide

Aleppo	uh LEP o
Alexandrinus	al'ig zan DRI nuhs
Anglican	ANG gli kuhn
Apocrypha	uh PAHK ri fuh, -ruh fuh
Aristeas	uh RIS ti ahs; ar is TEE uhs
Athanasius	ath uh NAY shi uhs, -shuhs
Augustine	AW guh steen; aw GUHS tuhn
Bezae	BEE zee
Byzantine	bi ZAN tin; BIZ uhn tin, -teen
Caesarean	ses uh REE uhn
canonicity	kan uh NISS uh tih
codex	KO deks
Constantine	KAHN stuhn tighn, -teen
cuneiform	kyoo NEE uh fawrm; KYOO nee uh fawrm
deuterocanoical	doo tuh roh kuh NAH nih kuhl
Diatessaron	digh uh TES uh rahn
Didache	DID uh kee
dittography	di TAHG ruh fi
Ephraemi	ee fruh mee
Erasmus	i RAZ muhs
Eusebius	yoo SEE bi uhs
genizah	guh NEET suh
Ignatius	ig NAY shi uhs, -shuhs
Irenaeus	irh ruh NEE uhs
Kethuvim	kuh THOO veem
Koine	koi NAY; KOI nay
Magdalen	MAG duh len, -lin, -luhn
Marcion	MAHR shuhn, -shi uhn
majuscules	mah JES skool
Masorah	muh SAWR uh
Masorete	MAS o reet
Masoretic	mas o RET ik, mas uh-
Megillot	mih GIL aht
Melito	MEL i to
minuscules	mi NUHS kyool
Muratorian	myoo ru TO ri uhn, -TAWR i uhn
Nevi'im	neh vih EEM

5

Origen	AHR i jen; AWR uh juhn
ostraca	AHS truh kuh
palimpsest	PAL imp sest
Papias	PAY pi uhs
papyrus	puh PIGH ruhs
papyri	puh PIGH ree, -righ
patristic	puh TRIS tik
Philo	FIGH lo
Polycarp	PAHL i kahrp
pseudpigrapha	syoo duh PIG ruh fuh
Qumran	kum RAHN
Septuagint	SEP tu uhn jint, -juhnt
Sinaiticus	sigh nay IT i kuhs
targums	TAHR guhm; tahr GOOM
Tatian	TAY shi uhn, -shuhn
Tanakh	TAH nahk; tah NAHK
Tertullian	tur TUHL i uhn
Textus Receptus	TEKS tuhs ri SEP thus
Tischendorf	TISH uhn dorf
Torah	TOH rah
Uncial	UHN shi uhl; UHN shuhl
Vaticanus	VAT ih KAN uhs
Vulgate	VUHL gayt
Wycliffe	WIK lif

References: White, Richard C, *The Vocabulary of the Church*. Macmillan Co., 1960; Severance, W. Murray, *Pronouncing Bible Names*, Expanded Ed. Broadman & Holman Publishers, 1994.

Lesson 1

The Bible: God's Revelation to Man

Introduction

The Bible claims that God revealed himself to man and that the Bible itself is the record of those revelations. These claims occur in all sections of the Bible. If these claims are true (as I believed they are), the Bible is divine in its origin.

The Old Testament Prophets

1. The OT Prophets claimed that the Lord spoke to them.

   a. The opening verses of Jeremiah are typical:

   *¹The words of Jeremiah, the son of Hilkiah, one of the priests who were in Anathoth in the land of Benjamin, ²to whom **the word of the LORD came** in the days of Josiah the son of Amon, king of Judah, in the thirteenth year of his reign. ³It came also in the days of Jehoiakim the son of Josiah, ...*

   *⁴Now **the word of the LORD came to me, saying,***

   *⁹ᵇAnd the LORD said to me, "Behold, **I have put my words in your mouth**.*

   *¹¹And the **word of the LORD came to me, saying,***

   *¹³The **word of the LORD came to me a second time, saying,***

   Later, Jeremiah is instructed to write these revelations in a book (Jer. 36).

   b. Two common phrases appear throughout the OT:

   "declares the Lord"   361 occurrences in ESV

   "says the Lord"   495 occurrences in ESV

   The consistent view of the OT is that God revealed his will through his Prophets. As we will see, this agrees with the view given in the NT.

The Testimony of Paul

The apostle Paul wrote 13 of the 27 books in the New Testament (14 if he wrote Hebrews). Within those writings, Paul attests to God's revelation.

Ephesians 3:1-7

¹For this reason I, Paul, a prisoner for Christ Jesus on behalf of you Gentiles – - ²assuming that you have heard of the stewardship of God's grace that was given to me for you, ³how the mystery was made known to me by revelation, as I have written briefly. ⁴When you read this, you can perceive my insight into the mystery of Christ, ⁵which was not made known to the sons of men in other generations as it has now been revealed to his holy apostles and prophets by the Spirit. ⁶This mystery is that the Gentiles are fellow heirs, members of the same body, and partakers of the promise in Christ Jesus through the gospel. ⁷Of this gospel I was made a minister according to the gift of God's grace, which was given me by the working of his power.

1. In this passage, what is the "*mystery*" that has been revealed?

2. How did Paul know of this mystery?

3. What is the process by which Paul came to know of this mystery?

4. How can we know of this mystery?

5. Why was Paul selected to receive this insight into this mystery? Was he the only one to receive this insight?

6. Compare Romans 16:25-27: *25"Now to him who is able to strengthen you according to my gospel and the preaching of Jesus Christ, according to the revelation of the mystery that was kept secret for long ages 26but has now been disclosed and through the prophetic writings has been made known to all nations, according to the command of the eternal God, to bring about the obedience of faith— 27to the only wise God be glory forevermore through Jesus Christ! Amen."*

1 Thessalonians 2:13

13And we also thank God constantly for this, that when you received the word of God, which you heard from us, you accepted it not as the word of men but as what it really is, the word of God, which is at work in you believers.

1. From whom does Paul claim to have received the message he preached?

2. Does Paul imply that he was faithful in presenting an accurate account of the message he received?

2 Timothy 3:14-16 (NKJV)

14But you must continue in the things which you have learned and been assured of, knowing from whom you have learned them, 15and that from childhood you have known the Holy Scriptures, which are able to make you wise for salvation through faith which is in Christ Jesus.

16All Scripture is given by inspiration of God, and is profitable for doctrine, for reproof, for correction, for instruction in righteousness, 17that the man of God may be complete, thoroughly equipped for every good work.

1. What two reasons does Paul give that lets Timothy be assured of the truthfulness of the things he has learned?

    1)

    2)

2. Consider the phrase "*All Scripture is given by inspiration of God*"?

    a. What does Paul mean by "*Scripture*"?

      Note "The designation 'Old Testament' is a Christian term that appeared at the end of the second century in Irenaeus and Tertullian to distinguish the Christian writings from those sacred writings preceding them." [McDonald, *Early Christianity*, 602]

    b. What is your understanding of the term "*inspiration*"? Be precise.

      What is your understanding of the above phrase?

    c. The translation "*inspiration*" (Gk. *theopneustos*) is a hangover from early English translations and is still used by many modern translations. More correctly, the Greek means "God-breathed" and, thus, refers to an *ex*-piration, not an *in*-spiration. Thus, the *English Standard Version* says, "*All Scripture is breathed out by God.*" Does this alter your understanding of the above phrase?

The Testimony of Peter

2 Peter 1:19-21

> *[19]And we have the prophetic word more fully confirmed, to which you will do well to pay attention as to a lamp shining in a dark place, until the day dawns and the morning star rises in your hearts, [20]knowing this first of all, that no prophecy of Scripture comes from someone's own interpretation. [21]For no prophecy was ever produced by the will of man, but men spoke from God as they were carried along by the Holy Spirit.*

1. What is the meaning of "*no prophecy of Scripture comes from someone's own interpretation*"? (CSB "No prophecy of Scripture comes from the prophet's own interpretation", NIV "no prophecy of Scripture came about by the prophet's own interpretation of things", NET "no prophecy of scripture ever comes about by the prophet's own imagination")

2. Why would Peter even need to say that prophecy did not come by the "*will of man*"?

3. What is the central teaching of this passage?

2 Peter 3:14-16

> [14]*Therefore, beloved, since you are waiting for these, be diligent to be found by him without spot or blemish, and at peace.* [15]*And count the patience of our Lord as salvation, just as our beloved brother Paul also wrote to you according to the wisdom given him,* [16]*as he does in all his letters when he speaks in them of these matters. There are some things in them that are hard to understand, which the ignorant and unstable twist to their own destruction, as they do the other Scriptures.*

1. Is this passage consistent with Paul's own writings? In what way?

2. What is the implication of the phrase "*the other Scriptures*"?

Conclusion

The Bible not only claims that God spoke to man, it also claims that it is the written record of God's revelations. Further, this written record is understandable, fully able to convey God's message.

Lesson 2

Ancient Writing

Introduction

The Bible is God's *written* word. Men wrote it using the common means available at the time. Ancient writing, like all writing, requires as a minimum a *writing medium* (the document material), an appropriate *writing implement*, and a *document form* (tablet, scroll, codex, etc.).

Writing Medium

Ancient documents used several different writing mediums: clay, stone, ivory, wood, wax, papyrus, leather, metal, and ostraca. The writing implement and document form had to be appropriate for the writing medium. The following chart summarizes the common relationships.

Writing Medium	Writing Implement	Document Form		
		Tablet	Scroll	Codex
Stone	Chisel, Reed	✓		
Wax	Stylus	✓		
Wood	Stylus	✓		
Clay	Stylus	✓		
Papyrus	Reed	✓	✓	✓
Leather	Reed	✓	✓	✓
Ostraca	Reed			

Stone   The hardness of stone materials varies greatly. Softer stones had obvious advantages as a writing material, but some uses, such as monument inscriptions, required harder stones for greater durability. Stone tablets were used (e.g., the Ten Commandments (Ex 24:12)), but other stone mediums such as the inside of cave walls or cliff-faces were also used for writing.

Wax   Waxed tablets were a common medium in Greece and Rome. Wax was placed within a shallow recess formed in a wood or ivory tablet. Writing was done by a stylus. Since the writing could easily be erased (smoothed), wax tablets were often used for temporary writings and personal correspondence. Since it is not very durable, as compared to clay, it is unknown how commonly it was used in ancient times.

Wood   "Over the past 30 years another type of wooden tablet has come to light. This is a very thin slat, like a piece of veneer; letters were incised on it with a sharp point and the slat folded in half, vertically. Then it was secured by a cord running through a V-shaped slot at each edge and tied. Scores of these slats, dating from AD 100, have been unearthed at Vindolanda, a fort on the frontier between Britain and Scotland where Hadrian's Wall was later erected... At other sites in Europe, additional examples of writing slats have been found, so it seems they were as common as wooden tablets." [Millard, "Writing Tablets", 40]

Clay   The oldest documents that have survived are written on clay. Clay mixed with limited amounts of water is pliable and can be shaped to the desired size, yet upon drying clay is remarkably durable. Clay documents were most often in the form of tablets, but they also took the form of prisms, cones or cylinders. Normally clay documents were air-dried, but some were baked for even greater durability. Clay was the only readily available material in Mesopotamia and was used for 3,000 years for cuneiform writing. Cuneiform script was impressed into the clay using a stylus.

Amarna Letter, Clay Tablet with Cuneiform Letters, Circa 1350 BCE. From Tell e-Amarna, Egypt. British Museum, London. ME 29788, July 23, 2016. Wikimedia Commons.

Papyrus   Papyrus (Lat. *papyrus*, Gk. *papuros*, Eng. *paper*) was crafted from the pith of a reed plant (also called papyrus) that predominantly grew in swamps along the Nile, with some presence in Palestine. "The pith of the reed was cut into strips about 12 to 15 inches long and laid in two layers, alternately horizontally and vertically. The sheets were left to dry on a flat surface with a weight on top, causing the natural sugar in the plant to bond the layers together" [Wegner, *Journey*, 92].

The front (*recto*) side with the horizontal strips was the primary writing surface, although at times, the back side (*verso*) was also used for writing. Writing on papyrus (and leather) was done with a reed and ink. The Egyptians used papyrus for over 4,000 years (3100 BC to AD 1000). Although papyrus was eventually used throughout the Greek and Roman world, the majority of recovered ancient papyri are from Egypt due to its dry climate. Presumably, most biblical manuscripts were originally written on papyrus.

Leather (Parchment, Vellum)   Animal skin (sheep, goats, cows, etc.) used for writing is sometimes differentiated into the categories leather, parchment, and vellum. Leather is prepared by tanning and has the lowest quality. Parchment and vellum, often used interchangeably but at times differentiated with vellum (originally referring to calfskin) being the highest quality, was generally prepared by soaking the skin in limewater, removing the hair, and then rubbing the skin with a pumice stone, although various other techniques were used. Animal skins are very durable and, tradition-ally, the Jews demanded that the Hebrew Scriptures be written on parchment.

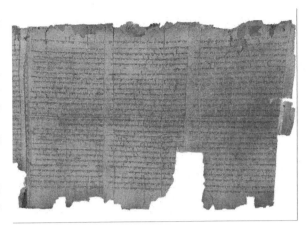

Portion of the Great Isaiah Scroll MS A (1 QIsa), Dead Sea Scrolls, 1ˢᵗ Century BCE, ink on Parchment, Discovered 1947 in Qumran Caves, 898208. Wikimedia Commons.

The cost of parchment is seen in that the "Codex Sinaiticus, ... a parchment manuscript that originally contained the entire Greek Bible, is estimated to have required the hides of approximately 360 sheep and goats" [Holmes, 126].

Ostraca   Ostraca refers to writing that was written on broken pottery (baked clay), so it is actually a document form, not a writing medium. It was commonly used for everyday purposes: grocery list, notes, etc.

Document Forms

Tablet   Tablets were probably the earliest document form used. Although readily available, they were not very convenient for larger documents. Clay tablets were often sealed within clay "envelopes" if privacy was desired.

Scroll   Individual sheets of papyrus or leather (parchment) could be joined together to form a scroll (Gk. *biblos* = Eng. *Book* = *Bible*). The typical papyrus scroll consisted of 20 sheets giving a length of about 14 feet. Writing was organized into columns. Jews still write the Torah with black ink on parchment scrolls.

> "The length of such a papyrus roll was limited by considerations of convenience in handling the roll; the normal Greek literary roll seldom exceeded 35 feet in length...The two longest books in the New Testament – the Gospel of Luke and the Book of Acts – would have filled an ordinary papyrus roll of 31 or 32 feet. Doubtless this is one of the reasons why Luke-Acts was issued in two volumes instead of one." [Metzger, *Text of the New Testament*, 5-6]

Codex   In ancient Roman usage, a codex was a wooden tablet used as a register. It became a technical term for any financial or authoritative collection of official or legal writings (hence, our word *code*). In modern usage, a codex refers to ancient documents of papyrus or parchment where the sheets are folded down the middle to form leaves, akin to the form of a modern book.

A Roman innovation, the codex swiftly gained favor among early Christians, with nearly all extant Christian writings from the early 2nd century onward adopting the codex format. Codices eventually replaced scrolls throughout the Roman world (about 50% of extant non-Christian writings from the 4th century are codices). [Alexander, "Ancient Book Production", 75]

The Case of Jeremiah

Jeremiah 36 offers a valuable illustration of how Jeremiah received the word of God and committed it to writing. Read the chapter carefully as you consider the following questions.

1. Who was asked by God to write all his words in a scroll? v.1

2. Who did Jeremiah get to actually write the words? v.4

3. So whose words were they? God's, Jeremiah's, or Baruch's?

4. What happen to the scroll Baruch wrote? v.20-24

5. So how do we still have a copy of Jeremiah? v.32

Bible Examples   For each of the passages, identify the writing medium, writing implement, and document form, if possible.

Biblical Passage	Writing Medium	Writing Implement	Document Form
Exodus 31:18 (24:12)			
Exodus 34:1, 27-28			
Joshua 8:32			
Job 19:23-24			
Isaiah 8:1			
Isaiah 30:8			
Isaiah 34:4			
Jeremiah 8:8			
Jeremiah 17:1			
Jeremiah 32:10			
Jeremiah 36:2-4, 18,23			
Ezekiel 2:9			
Ezekiel 9:2,3,11			
Ezekiel 37:16-20			
Habakkuk 2:2			
Luke 1:63			
2 Timothy 4:9, 13			
2 John 12; 3 John 13			

Lesson 3

Biblical Languages

Introduction

To the best of our knowledge, the Biblical books were originally written in Hebrew, Aramaic, and Greek. None of these languages are "dead" (as, for example, classical Latin is), rather all three are in use today. As with any living language, differences occur over time, "but there is much less difference between modern Hebrew and Biblical Hebrew, between modern Greek and Biblical Greek, than there is between modern English and English as spoken in 1066" [Bruce, *Books*, 24].

Hebrew

Hebrew is the language of the Old Testament (except for the few sections written in Aramaic noted below). Hebrew belongs to the Semitic (from Shem) family of languages, in particular the West Semitic branch containing Canaanite, Moabite, and Phoenician.

Note the following references (compare different translations):

Biblical Reference	Notes
Isaiah 19:18	
Isaiah 36:11	
Nehemiah 13:24	
Revelation 9:11	
Revelation 16:16	

1. The Hebrew alphabet contains 22 characters. Several of the Psalms are acrostic; that is, each verse begins with a different Hebrew letter. For example, Psalm 119 is composed of 22 sections with eight verses in each section. Each of the first eight verses begins with the first letter of the Hebrew alphabet, aleph; each of the second eight verses begins with the second letter of the Hebrew alphabet, bet; and so on. Compare the format of the Psalm 119 in various translations. Do the translations give any indication of this arrangement?

   [By the way, the word *alphabet* was formed by combining *aleph* and *bet*.]

2. Hebrew is written from right to left.

3. "During the Biblical period two different scripts were used for Hebrew, the earlier called paleo-Hebrew (or old Hebrew) and the later Square script (or Assyrian script after its origin...) ... Jesus was familiar with the Old Testament being written in Hebrew Square script when he said in Matthew 5:18, 'I tell you the truth, until heaven and earth disappear, not one *iota* or one *tittle*, will by any means disappear from the Law until everything is accomplished' (NIV, emphasis mine). The word *iota* is the Greek equivalent to the Hebrew letter *yod* ('), which is the smallest letter in Square script but not paleo-Hebrew script. The *tittle* is a small pen stroke that is used to help distinguish some letters (e.g., ד [*dalet*] and ר [*res*] are distinguished only by the small *tittle* on the top right-side corner of the *dalet*) and is not the same in paleo-Hebrew." [Wegner, *Journey*, 82, 85]

4. All 22 characters in the Hebrew alphabet represent consonants; the vowel sounds were left to the reader to supply. For a living language this may not be too difficult, but it is certainly easy to understand some resulting confusion. [*Note*: Biblical Hebrew has a vocabulary of about 8,000 words, with 90% of the text consisting of less than 2,000 words, whereas English has over 500,000.]

   a. Suppose we wrote English without vowels. What words could be represented by the word '*bd*'?

b. How about the phrase: th ct n th ht ?

Hebrew Alphabet		
'	aleph	א
b	beth	ב
g	gimmel	ג
d	daleth	ד
h	he	ה
w,v	waw	ו
z	zayin	ז
ch,ḥ	heth	ח
ṭ	teth	ט
y	yod	י
k	kaph	ך כ
l	lamed	ל
m	mem	ם מ
n	nun	ן נ
s	samekh	ס
ʻ	ayin	ע
p	pe	ף פ
ts	tsadhe	ץ צ
q	qoph	ק
r	resh	ר
sh	shin	ש
t	taw	ת

c. As an example, the word חרב (*ch-r-b*) in Deuteronomy 28:22 can either be understood as *sword* (Heb. *Chereb*; ASV, NASB, NET) or *drought* (Heb. *Choreb*; CEB, CSB, ESV, NABRE, NIV, NRSV) depending on which vowels were added. Which word do you think should be read based on the context?

d. As Hebrew speech passed out of daily use, it became necessary to indicate the proper vowels in the text. This was accomplished by the addition of vowel signs. Three different vowel systems have been discovered: the Babylonian, Palestinian, and Tiberian. The latter became the dominant system through the work of the Massoretes.

One interesting example involving vowel signs concerns the name of God. The Hebrew word (without vowels) is JHVH (or YHWH). In time, the Jews refused to say God's name out of reverence (or fear? cf. Ex.20:7). Instead, when reading the text, they would simply say the word *Lord* (Heb., *'Adonay*). Fourth Century and later manuscripts of the LXX began the practice of substituting the word 'Lord' for YHWH. The practice is continued by most English versions translating God's name as Lᴏʀᴅ. [Fitzmyer, *Spiritual Exercises*, 73]

As a reminder to the reader, the vowels of the word *Lord* (a-o-a) were indicated in the text above the name of God. Consequently, since the name of God had not been pronounced for a long period of time, no one knew the proper vowels to add. This has resulted with the hybrid English word *Jehovah* (the vowels of *Lord* inserted into the consonants for *God*) which was first used by William Tyndale in his English translation and adopted by the ASV. Many scholars today think the original Hebrew spelling for God was *Jahveh* (or *Yahweh*).

5. Because of the cost of making documents, ancient languages often employed a style called *scriptio continua* where the text was written with little, if any,

punctuation and without spaces between words [Witherington, 8]. At times, a single word would be broken onto two lines [Wurthwein, 108].

a. What are two possible understandings of the following sentence?

Godisnowhere

1)

2)

b. In Amos 6:12, for example, the text reads בבקרים which means "*with oxen (plural)*"; thus, the full expression literally reads "*Or does one plow with oxen?*" Since the context suggests that this is a rhetorical question that expects a "no" answer, the expression has been traditionally translated "*Or does one plow <u>there</u> with oxen?*" (ASV, NKJV, ESV, CSB, NLT). However, if a space is added in the text (thus, בבקר ים it now means "*the sea with oxen (collective)*"). The verse would then be translated as "*Or does one plow the sea with oxen?*" (NRSV, REB, NIV, NET). Any thoughts as to which is better?

Aramaic

Aramaic is also a Semitic language and "takes its name from the Arameans, or people of Aram.... Aram covered much of the upper Mesopotamia region and Aramaic became the international trade language...of the ancient Near East" [Wegner, *Journey*, 85-86]. The following sections of the Old Testament are written in Aramaic: Genesis 31:47 (the place-name "*Jegar Sahadutha*"); Jeremiah 10:11; Daniel 2:4b – 7:28; Ezra 4:8 – 6:18; 7:12-26.

1. In the eighth century BC, Aramaic became the diplomatic language used by Assyria. An interesting example of this is seen in 2 Kings 18:17-37 (cf. Is 36:2-22).

2. This diplomatic use of the Aramaic language continued with the Assyrians' successors: Babylon and Persia.

   a. The Aramaic section in Daniel begins with the magicians reply to Nebuchadnezzar. Read Daniel 2:4. The phrase "*in Aramaic*" probably should be understood as a note to the reader that the text starting at that point is in Aramaic and not that the magicians spoke in Aramaic.

   b. Also of significance, the words "*MENE, MENE, TEKEL, and PARSIN*" (Dan 5:25f) that were written on the wall during Belshazzar's feast were common Aramaic words for units of money or (with a different set of vowels) could be understood as *"numbered, weighed, and divided"* which is how Daniel used them in his interpretation.

    c. The sections of Ezra written in Aramaic contain several of the diplomatic letters written by Darius I and Artaxerxes I which would have been written in Aramaic.

3. During the exile, the displaced Jews no doubt became accustomed to speaking in Aramaic and the Jews who remained also lost some acquaintance with the Hebrew language because of their mixed marriages (Neh 13:24). Hence, Aramaic gradually displaced Hebrew so that by the time of Jesus Aramaic it is commonly assumed that Aramaic was the common language of Palestine. Interestingly, some scholars have suggested that some of the Gospels were first written in Aramaic, but there is no direct evidence to support this view. However, more recently, there appears to be growing evidence that Greek was a prevalent language of Galilee in the first century [Cleaves, *Did Jesus Speak Greek?*].

    a. Note the following Aramaic expressions and their translations in the New Testament:

Aramaic Expression	Biblical Reference	Translation
Talitha, cumi	Mark 5:41	
Ephphatha	Mark 7:34	
Eloi, Eloi, lama sabachthani	Mark 15:34	

As suggested by these references, Mark records the most Aramaisms of any Gospel. It would appear that Mark's readers do not know Aramaic (or probably Hebrew). This is consistent with the common view that Mark was writing for Christians in Rome. Of course, it would be consistent with any view that envisions the recipients as Greek readers.

b. Also, some Aramaic expressions found their way in the vocabulary of Hebrew and Greek (and even English). What do the following Aramaic words mean?

Aramaic Expression	Biblical Reference	Translation
Abba	Mark 14:36; Romans 8:15; Galatians 4:6	
Marana tha	1 Corinthians 16:22	
Mammon	Matthew 6:24	
Golgotha	John 19:17	

Greek

Greek, the language of the Aegean world, evolved through the centuries. Classical Greek, the language of Homer and Aristotle, is abundantly attested. After the conquests of Alexander the Great, Hellenistic Greek (also called *koine* Greek) became the official language of the lands surrounding the Mediterranean and loosely matches the language of the New Testament. But until the 1880s this form of Greek was unattested in the extant Greek literature of the ancient world. Consequently, some earlier scholars speculated that the Greek of the New Testament must have been some specially revealed language used by the Holy Spirit. However, the discovery of letters and other writings (especially the ostraca) of the common people demonstrated that the Greek of the New Testament was simply a manifestation of the common vernacular [Bruce, *Books*, 53-56].

Greek Alphabet

a	alpha	A	α	n	nu	N	ν
b	beta	B	β	x	xi	Ξ	ξ
g	gamma	Γ	γ	o	omikron	O	o
d	delta	Δ	δ	p	pi	Π	π
e	epsilon	E	ε	r	rho	P	ρ
z	zeta	Z	ζ	s	sigma	Σ	σ
ē	eta	H	η	t	tau	T	τ
th	theta	Θ	θ	u,y	upsilon	Y	υ
i	iota	I	ι	ph	phi	Φ	φ
k	kappa	K	κ	ch	chi	X	χ
l	lamda	Λ	λ	ps	psi	Ψ	ψ
m	mu	M	μ	ō	omega	Ω	ω

The pervasiveness of Greek allowed the gospel to be preached by the apostles throughout the Roman Empire with no language barriers. To the best of our knowledge, all the New Testament books were originally written in koine Greek with the few Aramaic words noted above. [However, Papias, as quoted by Eusebius, notes that Matthew was written in the 'Hebrew dialect'. Consequently, there have been a few scholars who have argued that Matthew was first written in Hebrew (or Aramaic) and then translated into Greek, but it does not appear to be commonly held.]

1. The Greek alphabet was derived from the Phoenician alphabet (which is very similar to Hebrew). Koine Greek has 24 letters in its alphabet with *alpha* being the first and *omega* the last (compare Rev 22:1).

2. Earlier forms of Greek were written from right to left like Hebrew, but after 500 BC Greek was written left to right.

   The lack of punctuation can lead to ambiguous meanings. For example, John 7:37b-38 is rendered by the ESV (following most earlier English versions):

   "If anyone thirsts, let him come to me and drink. Whoever believes in me, as the Scripture has said, 'Out of his heart will flow rivers of many waters.'"

Alternately, the CEB translates:

"All who are thirsty come to me! All who believe in me should drink! As the scriptures said concerning me, Rivers of living water will flow from within him."

Which do you think is correct?

Transliterated Words

Similar to other modern languages, English has adopted several foreign words directly by transliteration instead of translation. That is, they simply kept the basic spelling of the word. Examples are:

1. *Amen*, common also with Hebrew, Greek and Late Latin, means "it is so" or "so be it".

2. *Anathema,* used in the KJV (1 Cor 16:22) and the ASV (also Rom 9:3; 1 Cor 12:3; Gal 1:8, 9) but not in the ESV, means "thing devoted (to evil)".

3. *Baptize*, from Greek, means "to dip, bathe". (Alexander Campbell's translation, *The Living Oracles*, and the recent *International English Bible* are unique in that they always used forms of *immerse* in lieu of *baptize*.)

Lesson 4

Old Testament Canon

Introduction

"When we speak of the canon of scripture, the word 'canon' has a simple meaning. It means the list of books contained in scripture; the list of books recognized as worthy to be included in the sacred writings of a worshipping community... The word 'canon' has come into our language (through Latin) from the Greek word *kanon*. In Greek it meant a rod, especially a straight rod used as a rule; from this usage comes the other meaning which the word commonly bears in English – 'rule' or 'standard'. We speak, for example, of the 'canons' or rules of the Church of England. But a straight rod might be marked in units of length (like a modern ruler marked in inches or centimeters); from this practice the Greek word *kanon* came to be used of the series of such marks, and hence to be used in the general sense of 'series' or 'list'. It is this last usage that underlies the term 'the canon of scripture'." [Bruce, *Canon*, 17-18]

Hebrew Bible

1. Traditionally, the Hebrew Bible contained 24 books and was divided into three sections: the Law (Torah), the Prophets (Nevi'im), and the Writings (Kethuvim); thus, the Jews called their sacred writings the Tanakh (an acronym: TaNaKh).

    Law   Or, **Books of Moses**, **Pentateuch** (*Gk* 'five-volumes'): Genesis, Exodus, Leviticus, Numbers, Deuteronomy

    Prophets   *Former*:   Joshua, Judges, Samuel, Kings
    Latter: Isaiah, Jeremiah, Ezekiel, Book of the Twelve

    Writings   Psalms, Proverbs, Job
    The Scrolls (*Megillot*): Song of Songs, Ruth, Lamentations, Ecclesiastes, Esther
    Daniel, Ezra-Nehemiah, Chronicles

    The order given above is that given in the Masoretic text (see Lesson 6). The order of some prophetic books and those among the Writings varied in Jewish accounts (see below). This probably reflects the fact that these books were scrolls which inherently have no order.

The traditional titles of many of the books of Tanakh are derived from the first word in the book. For example, Genesis is titled *Bereshith* ("In the beginning"), Exodus is *We-elleh shemoth* ("These are the names"), etc. The names we know (Genesis, Exodus, etc.) come from the Septuagint (see below).

a. Parallel passages in the Gospels (Mt 23:34-35//Lk 11:49-51) record Jesus' statement that the Jewish nation will be held responsible for the blood of the prophets from *"the blood of Abel"* (recorded in Gen 4:8) to the *"blood of Zechariah"* (recorded in 2 Chr 24:20-22). It seems that Jesus was intending to place the blood of all the Old Testament martyrs upon the heads of the Jews. But chronologically, Zechariah is not the last martyr of the Old Testament; Uriah was killed nearly two hundred years after Zechariah (Jer 26:20-23). So, why might have Jesus named Zechariah instead of Uriah?

b. The three-fold division of the Hebrew Bible is possibly reflected in Jesus' statement in Luke 24:44 (NIV): *"This is what I told you while I was still with you: Everything must be fulfilled that is written about me in the Law of Moses, the Prophets, and the Psalms."* Why might the third section of the Hebrew Bible be called the Psalms?

Of course, some scholars deny that the reference to Psalms is a reference to the entire third section of the Hebrew Bible. These scholars generally deny that the Hebrew canon was closed in the first century.

c. On other occasions, the whole Hebrew Bible is referred to by *"Moses and all the prophets"* (Lk 24:27), *"the law and the prophets"* (Mt 7:12; Rom 3:21), or by just *"the law"* (Jn 10:34; Rom 3:10-19; 1 Cor 14:21). Regardless of the description, do these passages seem to refer to a definite collection of writings? In other words, is a *canon* of writings being referred to? Consider the reference by Jesus to *"all the Scriptures"* (Lk 24:27).

2. Extrabiblical Jewish Evidence for an Old Testament Canon

   a. Joshua ben Sira (*Gk.* Jesus the Son of Sirach), a scribe, wrote a book of wisdom called *Ecclesiasticus* (or *Sirach* or *The Wisdom of Jesus the Son of Sirach*) between 196 and 175 BC. His grandson translated the original Hebrew book into Greek sometime after 132 BC and added a prologue in which he refers to "the Law and the Prophets and the others (*mg.* 'other books') that followed them" as "scriptures" (NRSV). [deSilva, *Introducing the Apocrypha*, 158]

   b. Josephus writes (AD 90s):

   "It therefore naturally, or rather necessarily, follows (seeing that with us it is not open to everybody to write the records, and that there is no discrepancy in what is written; seeing that, on the contrary, the prophets alone had this privilege, obtaining their knowledge of the most remote and ancient history through the inspiration which they owed to God, and committing to writing a clear account of the events of their own time just as they occurred) – it follows, I say, that we do not possess myriads of inconsistent books conflicting with each other. Our books, those which are justly accredited, are but two and twenty, and contain the record of all time.

   "Of these, five are the books of Moses, comprising the laws and traditional history from the birth of man down to the death of the lawgiver.... the prophets subsequent to Moses wrote the history of the events of their own times in thirteen books. The remaining four books contain hymns to God and precepts for the conduct of human life.

   "From Artaxerxes to our own time a complete history has been written, but has not been deemed worthy of equal credit with the earlier records, because of the failure of the exact succession of prophets.

   "We have given practical proof of our reverence for our own Scriptures. For although such long ages have now passed, no one has ventured either to alter a syllable; and it is an instinct with every Jew, from the day of his birth to regard them as the decrees of God, to abide by them, and, if need be, cheerfully to die for them." [*Contra Apion* 1.37-42, quoted by Wegner, *Journey*, 117]

   Bruce observes that the 22 books of Josephus is probably the 24 books of the Hebrew Bible with "Ruth being counted as an appendix to Judges and Lamentations to Jeremiah" [*Canon*, 33], and that Josephus may have arranged the books into 22 to agree with the number of letters in the Hebrew alphabet [*Books*, 90].

c. The apocryphal book of 2 Esdras was written (as generally agreed) after the destruction of Jerusalem but presumably records revelations made to Ezra after the destruction of Solomon's temple. By divine illumination, Ezra dictates 94 books to five scribes over a period of 40 days.

> *And when the forty days were ended, the Most High spoke to me, saying, "Make public the twenty-four books that you wrote first, and let the worthy and the unworthy read them; but keep the seventy that were written last, in order to give them to the wise among your people..."* [2 Esdras 14:45-46 NRSV]

Apparently, the first 24 books were the accepted books of the Hebrew Bible.

d. Following the destruction of Jerusalem, a group of Jewish rabbis around AD 90-100 set up headquarters at Jabeh or Jamnia in western Judaea to discuss how to conduct religious life in the wake of the temple's destruction. Among their subjects of discussions were the Hebrew Scriptures and other Jewish writings. For various reasons, questions were raised concerning Ezekiel, Proverbs, Song of Solomon, Ecclesiastes, and Esther. However, they concluded that these books did not contradict any other accepted Scriptures and thus should be accepted as Scripture. It does not appear that these rabbis fixed the limits of the OT canon (as some contend), rather they simply reaffirmed the canon as they had received it.

e. The Dead Sea Scrolls discovered at Qumran, northwest of the Dead Sea, include about 100 complete texts or fragments of all the OT Books except Esther. But there are about 400 other documents contained in the Qumran collection, and there are no definitive statements by the men of Qumran as to which were considered Scripture. There are general statements within their commentaries suggesting that they considered the books contained within the Law and the Prophets as Scripture along with Psalms, Daniel, and, possibly, Job. One interesting statement in the document identified as 4QMMT (written around 150 BC) is:

> [And] we have [also written] to you so that you may have understanding in the book of Moses [and] in the book[s of the Pr]ophets and in Davi[d and in the events] of ages past... [Vanderkam, 170; portions included in brackets are missing and thus is the best guess at what was written.]

Although fragmentary, this appears to reflect at least a three-fold division of the Old Testament with "David" representing at least the Psalms and, possibly, the entire group of the Writings (compare Lk 24:44, see above).

3. Extrabiblical Christian Evidence for an Old Testament Canon

    a. The first dateable Christian list of OT books is attributable to Melito, bishop of Sardis in about AD 170 who claims to have accurately obtained it while traveling in Syria. His list contains all the books of the Hebrew Bible except Esther (assuming that he included Lamentations with Jeremiah).

    b. Origen (AD 185-254) lists 22 books of the OT Canon that is the same as the 24 books of the Hebrew Bible (with Ruth and Lamentations being included with Judges and Jeremiah, respectively). Origen also includes the 'Letter of Jeremiah', an apocryphal writing, with Jeremiah.

    c. Athanasius, bishop of Alexandria, also mentions in a letter dated AD 367 the 22 books of the OT, but he arrives at 22 by separating Ruth from Judges and omitting Esther. He also includes the apocryphal book 'Baruch' along with Jeremiah-Lamentations-Letter of Jeremiah.

    d. Jerome, in his Prologue to the Books of Samuel and Kings, "remarks that in some Jewish circles the number of books was reduced to twenty-two to correspond with the number of letters in the Hebrew alphabet, by counting Ruth along with Judges and Lamentations along with Jeremiah; while in others the number was raised to twenty-seven (to allow for those letters of the alphabet, five in number, which have two forms each), by dividing Samuel, Kings, Chronicles, Ezra-Nehemiah and Jeremiah-Lamentations into two books each." [Bruce, *Books*, 92-93]

Septuagint

Upon conquering Egypt, Alexander the Great founded the city of Alexandria in 331 BC and it became the capital of the kingdom of the Ptolemies who succeeded to Alexander's empire in Egypt. Soon after its founding, Alexandria became home to a significant Jewish settlement (recall that a large group of Jews went to Egypt following the destruction of Jerusalem by Nebuchadnezzar in 587 BC). Over time, the Jews began to speak Greek only, which necessitated a Greek translation of the Hebrew Bible. During the period 250-100 BC, Greek versions of Hebrew Bible appeared. It appears that the five books of the Law were the first to be translated since these related to the Jewish worship and the term Septuagint was first given to a Greek version of the Law.

In the course of time a legend attached itself to this Greek version of the law, telling how it was the work of seventy or rather seventy-two elders of Israel who were brought to Alexandria for the purpose. It is because of this legend that the term Septuagint (from Latin *septuaginta*, 'seventy') came to be attached to the version. As time went on, the term came to be attached to the whole of the Old Testament in Greek, and the original legend of the seventy was further embellished. The legend is recorded originally in a document called the *Letter of Aristeas*, which tells how the elders completed the translation of the Pentateuch in seventy-two days, achieving an agreed version as the result of regular conference and comparison. Later embellishments not only extended their work to cover the whole Old Testament but told how they were isolated from one another in separate cells for the whole period and produced seventy-two identical versions – conclusive proof, it was urged, of the divine inspiration of the work! Philo, the Jewish philosopher of Alexandria, relates how the translators worked in isolation from one another but wrote the same text word for word, 'as though it were dictated to each by an invisible prompter'; but both he and Josephus confirm that it was only the books of the law that were translated by the elders. It was Christian writers who extended their work to the rest of the Old Testament and, taking over Philo's belief in their inspiration, extended that also to cover the whole of the Greek Old Testament, including those books that never formed part of the Hebrew Bible. [Bruce, *Canon*, 44]

1. The books of the Septuagint are:

    Law   Genesis, Exodus, Leviticus, Numbers, Deuteronomy

    History   Joshua, Judges, Ruth, Books of the Kingdom (1 Reign (1 Sam), 2 Reign (2 Sam), 3 Reign (1 Kings), and 4 Reign (2 Kings)), Books of Chronicles (1 & 2), *1 Esdras*, 2 Esdras (Ezra-Nehemiah), Esther (with *The Additions to the Book of Esther*), *Judith*, *Tobit*

    Poetry & Wisdom Psalms (plus *Psalm 151*), Proverbs, Ecclesiastes, Song of Songs, Job, *Wisdom, Ecclesiasticus*

    Prophets   The Twelve, Isaiah, Jeremiah, Lamentations, *Baruch, Letter of Jeremiah*, Ezekiel, *Susanna* – Daniel – *The Prayer of Azariah and the Song of Three Men* – *Bel and the Dragon*

    Appendix   *Books of Maccabees (1, 2)*

2. The order of our English OT (as well as the titles of our OT books) generally follows the Septuagint (through the Latin Vulgate), except that the twelve Minor Prophets follow the Major Prophets. However, the location of The Twelve and even other books varied in different Septuagint manuscripts.

3. The additional books of the Septuagint not found in the Hebrew Bible (italicized in the list above and sometimes called the *Septuagint plus*), along with *2 Esdras* (not the same as above) and *The Prayer of Manasseh*, formed what is called the *Apocrypha*. There are other Jewish writings, called the *pseudepigrapha* ('false subscriptions'), that generally purports to have been written by Old Testament characters, but which have never been considered canonical by any group.

4. Except for a few fragments, the earliest extant copies of the Septuagint come from Christian sources of the fourth and fifth century. Consequently, the question arises whether the books of the Septuagint plus were originally included by Jews,

or later by Christians, and, were they included because they were considered Scripture.

Canonicity of the Apocrypha

1. Jewish Sources

    a. Philo (20 BC – AD 50), an Alexandrian Jew who used the Septuagint, clearly acknowledges the books of the Hebrew Bible that he quotes as possessing divine authority (he quotes all the books of the Law, most of the Prophets, and many of the Writings). Yet he never quotes one of the books in the *Septuagint plus*.

    b. Josephus, too, used the Septuagint, but (as noted above) he gave authoritative status to the 24 books of the Hebrew Bible that he did not accord to other writings.

2. New Testament

    a. All the New Testament writers use the Septuagint to some degree and it is the basis of most of the Old Testament quotations in the New Testament writings. In many instances, New Testament writers clearly acknowledge the authority of the books of the Hebrew Bible.

    b. There is no instance in which they quote from one of the *Septuagint plus* as Scripture. There appear to be a few allusions to the *Septuagint plus* and the pseudepigrapha (even a quotation of pseudepigraphal book *1 Enoch* occurs in Jude 14f), but they are not identified, or appealed to, as Scripture.

3. Early Church

    a. The Christian use of the Septuagint became so widespread that the Jews stopped using the Septuagint and began using other Greek translations of the Hebrew Bible, particularly the one produced by Aquila.

    b. Generally speaking, the early church fathers (e.g., Origen, Tertullian, and Augustine) accepted all the Septuagint (and even some pseudepigrapha) as Scripture. Although some (such as Justin Martyr) consider the Septuagint to be superior to the Hebrew Bible, most seem to give priority to the Hebrew Bible for those books of the Septuagint contained within the Hebrew Bible.

    c. One notable exception to this consensus was Jerome, the author of the Latin Vulgate. Jerome uses the Hebrew Bible as the basis of the Vulgate, but also includes translations for the *Septuagint plus* (at the request of his friend Augustine [Armstrong, 121]). However, he is careful to note in his prologues that the Apocrypha (the term originating with Jerome and means 'hidden') are not on the same level as Scripture, although they may have some ethical value.

    d. Consequently, Roman Catholics accept the books of the *Septuagint plus* (except *1 Esdras*) as *Deuterocanonical* ("second canon") as decreed by the Council of Trent in 1546.

    e. The Greek Orthodox Church accepts all the books of the *Septuagint plus* and *1 Esdras*, *The Prayer of Manasseh*, *Psalm 151*, and *3 & 4 Maccabees* as Deuterocanonical.

    f. Protestants at the time of the Reformation reexamined the question of canon and generally considered the additional books as Apocryphal, thus not to be used for doctrine. Yet, Lutherans and Anglicans continued to use them for their ethical value.

    g. All the early English translations (including the King James Version) contained the Apocrypha.

Hebrew Bible	Septuagint (LXX)	
		Septuagint plus
Law	**Law**	
Genesis	Genesis	
Exodus	Exodus	
Leviticus	Leviticus	
Numbers	Numbers	
Deuteronomy	Deuteronomy	
Prophets	**History**	
Former:	Joshua	
Joshua	Judges	
Judges	Ruth	
Samuel	Books of the Kingdoms	
Kings	(Samuel-Kings)	
	Books of Chronicles	
Latter:		*1 Esdras*
Isaiah	2 Esdras	
Jeremiah	Esther	*Additions to Esther*
Ezekiel		*Judith*
Book of the Twelve		*Tobit*
Writings	**Poetry & Wisdom**	
Psalms	Psalms	*Psalm 151*
Proverbs	Proverbs	
Job	Ecclesiastes	
The Scrolls:		
Song of Songs	Song of Songs	
Ruth	Job	*Wisdom*
Lamentations		*Ecclesiasticus*
Ecclesiastes		
Esther	**Prophets**	
Daniel		
Ezra-Nehemiah	The Twelve	
Chronicles	Isaiah	
	Jeremiah	
	Lamentations	
		Baruch
		Letter of Jeremiah
	Ezekiel	
	Daniel	*Susanna*
		Prayer of Azariah
		Song of Three Men
		Bel and the Dragon
		Appendix: Books of Maccabees

Note: Apocrypha = Septuagint plus + 2 Esdras +
Prayer of Manasseh

Lesson 5

New Testament Canon

Introduction

To the best of our knowledge, the 27 books that make up our New Testament were not a single collection during the lives of the apostles. So, the canon of the New Testament grew as books were circulated and acknowledged to be authoritative. As this lesson will suggest, this process began in the first century.

New Testament Evidence

1. The apostles claimed to be speaking (and, thus writing) with authority from God:

   a. Acts 15:1-29 (esp. v.7 & 12)
   b. Acts 22:14-15
   c. Romans 1:1-5 (Typical of Paul's opening salutation)
   d. 1 Corinthians 1:17; 2:1-4
   e. 1 Corinthians 15:1-11
   f. Galatians 1:8
   g. Ephesians 3:1-7
   h. Colossians 1:25
   i. 1 Thessalonians 2:4
   j. 1 Peter 1:10-12
   k. 2 Peter 1:16-21

2. There appears to be some desire on Paul's part to have his teachings preserved:

   a. 1 Corinthians 11:2
   b. 2 Thessalonians 2:15

3. There is the clear indication that Paul's letters were for all Christians:

   a. 1 Thessalonians 5:27
   b. Colossians 4:16

4. New Testament books written later quote from New Testament books written earlier as Scripture:

   a. 1 Timothy 5:18 quotes Deuteronomy 25:4 and Luke 10:7

   b. 2 Peter 3:15-16 (In addition, this text suggests that Peter was familiar with a *collection* of Paul's letters.)

Testimony of the Early Church Fathers

The early church fathers acknowledged the authority of Jesus and the apostles.

1. Clement of Rome, in his letter to the Corinthian church (c 96), quotes from the Sermon on the Mount and gives authority to the words of Jesus as he does the Old Testament prophets.

2. Ignatius, bishop of Antioch (c 110), argues that "gospel" containing the words of Jesus are Scripture like the Old Testament Scriptures.

3. The Didache (100-150?) quotes the Lord's Prayer that the writer says the Lord commanded in his Gospel.

4. Polycarp writes the church at Philippi between 110 and 120 and reminds them of what is said in Scripture by quoting two statements from Ephesians 4.

5. Basilides, a gnostic contemporary of Polycarp, precedes a quote from Romans 8 with "as it is written" and refers to a verse in 1 Corinthians 2 as "the scripture."

6. The writer of Second Clement (2nd Century), after quoting Isaiah, quotes Matthew with the statement "And another scripture says..."

7. The Letter of Barnabas (2nd Century) introduces a quote from Matthew with "as it is written."

The Gospels

One of the earliest collections of multiple New Testament writings was the fourfold gospel.

1. Papias, bishop of Hierapolis (c 125), knew of Matthew's and Mark's Gospels, but he does not indicate whether they were part of a collection. He says that Mark was the interpreter of Peter.

2. Justin Martyr (c 140-160) may be the first to allude to a collection of the Gospels when he speaks of the 'memoirs' of Peter (possibly the Gospel of Mark) and the "memoirs of the apostles" which, he says, were called Gospels.

3. Tatian, Justin's disciple, compiled the first known harmony of the four Gospels (after 165) in a work called *Diatessaron* ('harmony of four'). This work is known to have circulated in both Greek and Syriac.

4. Without doubt, the codex form popularized by the early Christians lent itself to collecting the four Gospels together. The fragments of a codex manuscript (P^{75}) from the late 2nd or early 3rd century contain Luke and John, but probably was a codex of all four Gospels. The earliest surviving codex of all four Gospels (and Acts!) is from the early 3rd century.

The Pauline Corpus

1. When Clement of Rome sent his letter to the church of Corinth (96), he had a copy of 1 Corinthians (and other letters of Paul?).

2. Polycarp in his letter to the church at Philippi refers to the "letters" that Paul had written them. Based on his writings, it appears that he knew all of Paul's letters except Colossians, 1 Thessalonians, Philemon, and Titus. [Wegner, *Journey*, 137].

3. The earliest surviving codex of the Pauline corpus (P^{46}; except the Pastorals) was written about 200.

4. From the early 2nd century, all Christian writers knew of Paul's letters as a collection.

5. Marcion published his collection of Paul's letters (which he named *Apostle*) about 144.

Early Lists of the New Testament

As in the above references, most of our knowledge of which books were considered authoritative among the early Christians is obtained from their writings in which they quote various New Testament books. As time progressed, some writers purposefully listed and discussed the books accepted as Scripture.

1. The Muratorian Canon refers to a list of books accepted as Scripture that was composed about 190 and was found in an 8th century Latin manuscript by Cardinal Muratori. The list "does not mention Hebrews, James, 1 & 2 Peter, and 3 John. Extra books that [it] includes are the Wisdom of Solomon and Revelation of Peter, stating that some do not accept the latter" [Wegner, *Journey*, 142]. Further, it is clear in excluding a writing entitled the *Shepherd of Hermas* as canonical.

2. Eusebius gathered from the writings of Origen (185-254) a list of 21 books that were accepted by Christians. The six disputed books were Hebrews, James, 2 Peter, 2 & 3 John, and Jude. Origen is the first Christian to mention 2 Peter. At one time he seemed to acknowledge the Didache, the Letter of Barnabas, and the Shepherd of Hermas as Scripture, but later questions them.

3. Eusebius of Caesarea (the historian) divides the early writings into three categories: the universally accepted, the disputed, and the spurious books. Among the disputed are James, Jude, 2 Peter, 2 & 3 John, although he acknowledges that the majority accepts them. He counts as spurious the Acts of Paul, the Shepherd of Hermas, the Apocalypse of Peter, the Didache, and the Letter of Barnabas. Interestingly, he lists Revelation both as universally accepted and as spurious.

4. Athanasius, bishop of Alexandria, in 367 listed exactly the 27 books of our New Testament as those acknowledged as Scripture. After this, there was still some differences of opinion in various churches, but within a fairly short time it seems that the 27 books were universally accepted.

5. To the best of our knowledge, the Council of Hippo (393) was probably the first church council to define the limits of Scripture. It was closely followed by the Third Council of Carthage (397). Both limit the canon to the 27 books we recognize as Scripture.

The Criteria of Canonicity

As judgments were being made regarding which writings were canonical, what criteria did the early Christians use to differentiate? Based on the writings of the early Christians, the following have been suggested [cf. Bruce, *Canon*, 255ff]:

1. *Apostolic Authority.* Undoubtedly, this was the major test since the apostles were acknowledged messengers of Christ.

2. *Antiquity.* If the writing was authored by an apostle (or one closely associated) with an apostle, then it follows that the writing must belong to the apostolic age.

3. *Orthodoxy.* Scripture should be consistent with Scripture; thus, any given writing could be compared with accepted Scripture.

4. *Catholicity.* Assurance of the authoritative nature of a writing could in some measure be based on how widely accepted the writing was.

5. *Traditional Use.* Similarly, if a writing from an early date was traditionally accepted as an authoritative writing, it would be difficult to deny the tradition.

6. *Inspiration.* The ultimate question was whether the writer received a revelation from God. This implies that others besides the apostles could be the writer of a canonical work.

Thought Questions

1. There are two letters that Paul wrote that we do not have copies of: (1) the letter to the Corinthians that preceded 1 Corinthians (1 Cor 5:9), and (2) the letter to the Laodiceans (Col 4:16). Suppose archaeologists uncovered an ancient document that purported to be a copy of one of these letters.

   a. Could we determine whether it was genuine?

   b. If we did agree it was genuine, could we add it to the New Testament canon?

   c. Or, do you think it is impossible for copies of these letters to exist? If so, why?

   d. Is it possible that the judgment of the early Christians is wrong? Are we obligated to make our own judgments on which books should be in the canon?

2. Did Paul understand that a collection would be made? Some NT scholars even think Paul himself kept a collection of his writings that may have accelerated them being circulated [Trobisch [*Paul's Letter Collection*]. But, even if not, does that speak against the validity of making a collection?

A Counterview

Some scholars [e.g., Bart Ehrman, *Lost Christianities;* Gerd Lüdemann, *Heretics*] think the canon of the New Testament simply represents the views of that group of Christians who prevailed in the early centuries of Christianity. In this view, there were many competing forms of Christianity in the early centuries with each being as valid as the others. Thus, the writings we refer to as the New Testament are no more special than many other writings in those early centuries. Rather, they are simply those writings favored by the predominant form of Christianity.

One writing that gets a lot of attention, some calling it the Fifth Gospel, is the *Gospel of Thomas* (part of the Nag Hammadi library discovered in 1945), which is basically a random collection of sayings attributed to Jesus. Some of these sayings are similar to those in the canonical Gospels, whereas others are unique. Could it be that some of these sayings are genuine? Perhaps, but that does not mean the *Gospel of Thomas* should be included in the canon. What these scholars refuse to acknowledge is the possibility that God revealed his will to men and women. As seen at the first of this lesson, the writers of the New Testament books claim to have received that revelation, and that is the primary reason Christians have acknowledged these books as authoritative.

Lesson 6

Old Testament Text

Introduction

None of the original manuscripts, called the autographs, of the Biblical texts are in our possession. Presumably, they have perished long ago. Consequently, the oldest Hebrew and Greek texts we possess are copies of copies. This naturally raises questions concerning the accuracy of these copies. How faithful do they represent the autographs? What corruptions to the text have occurred? And how do we identify these corruptions? The field of study called Textual Criticism seeks to answer these questions. [In past generations, Textual Criticism was called Lower Criticism in contrast to the Higher Criticism that questioned the integrity of the text and the authors of Scripture.] In addition to the Hebrew texts themselves, early translations of the Hebrew texts such as the Septuagint, the Aramaic targums, and the Latin Vulgate provide witness to the Hebrew texts.

Hebrew Texts of the Old Testament

1. The standard modern Hebrew text of the Old Testament is the *Biblia Hebraica Stuttgartensia* edited by Elliger and Rudolph, which is based on the *Codex Leningradensis* (L) (dated 1008) that was discovered in the 19th century. Another modern text, the *Hebrew University Bible*, is based on the *Aleppo Codex* (A) that dates from the first half of the 10th century, but it was partially destroyed in the Jewish riots of 1947 and 1948.

2. Both of these Hebrew codices are representative of the Masoretic Text (MT) which is the traditional text preserved by the Jews. It is believed that after the destruction of Jerusalem (AD 70) Jewish scholars produced a standard consonantal text of the Hebrew Scriptures by about 100. No complete texts have survived from this period because it was the Jewish practice to destroy older, worn-out copies due to their desire to keep them out of unholy hands. They would temporarily store older copies in a *genizah* (Heb. 'hiding place') – a room adjoining the synagogue – until they were taken to consecrated ground for burial.

3. The consonantal text was supplemented by the Masoretes with the *Masorah* (Heb. 'tradition'), that is, a system of signs indicating punctuation and vowels (since Hebrew was no longer a living vernacular) as well as marginal notes. The Masoretes did their work from about 500 to 1000. There were three schools of Masoretes: Palestinian, Tiberian, and Babylonian, but ultimately the authoritative Masorah was the result of the ben Asher family (750 – 950) in Tiberias. The *Aleppo Codex* noted above was the work of Aaron ben Moses ben Asher, the last surviving member of the ben Asher family. In 895, his father, Moses ben Asher, wrote and pointed the *Codex Cairensis* (C), which contains the Former and Latter Prophets.

> "The effect of the Masorah was to ensure remarkably accurate transmission of the text, including its inherent anomalies and discrepancies... The text was sacred, not a perceived understanding of it, and a scribe was to be neither more nor less than a scribe, no matter how creative or how careless he might be. Unique or rare formulations of words or phrases, especially those vulnerable to error, were noted so that the next scribe would not change them to more familiar or more understandable forms... The Masorah, moreover, provides statistics of the number of verses, of lectionary sections, and of words, even noting what word or letter is precisely in the middle of a book or section, so that the next scribe would have full means of guarding the integrity of each letter, each word, each particular phrase, and hence each book that was his charge to copy." [Sanders, "Masorah", 501]

4. "There are thirty-one extant Masoretic manuscripts of the Hebrew Bible, complete or fragmentary, dating from the late 9th century to 1100 CE, and some three thousand thereafter." [Sanders, *ibid*, 501]

5. After the invention of the printing press, a Hebrew Bible, called the *Second Rabbinic Bible*, produced by Jacob ben Chayyim, a Jewish Christian, was published in 1524/25 and became the standard printed text of the Hebrew Bible until the 20th century. This edition was based on 12th century manuscripts of the MT.

6. Other Hebrew manuscripts:

   a. The oldest Hebrew texts are on the Silver Amulets found in 1985 and dated to mid-7th century BC. These amulets (which are charms against evil) were probably worn as a necklace or bracelet and contain a copy of Numbers 6:22-27: *"The Lord bless you and keep you, the Lord make his face shine upon you and be gracious unto you, the Lord lift his countenance upon you and give you peace."*

   b. Prior to the discovery of the Dead Sea Scrolls, the oldest Hebrew manuscript was the Nash Papyrus (acquired in 1902 by W.L. Nash) that contained a damaged copy of the Decalogue. It has been dated anywhere from 170 BC to AD 70.

c. The Dead Sea Scrolls contain Hebrew biblical manuscripts that are 1,000 years older than any previous known Hebrew manuscripts. This is exactly the type of information needed to determine how much variance occurred in the Hebrew text over the 1,000-year interim. Interestingly, some of these manuscripts (e.g., the second scroll of Isaiah) substantially agree with the MT confirming the care the Masoretes took in transmitting the text. Of course, there are other Hebrew manuscripts that deviate from the MT which suggests the existence of multiple text types prior to the uniformity imposed by the Masoretes.

d. The Cairo Genizah fragments were discovered in the 19th century in a genizah that had been built over and apparently forgotten. About 200,000 fragments of manuscripts were retrieved; 30,000 of which were Biblical texts in Hebrew, Aramaic, or Arabic. The earliest Hebrew fragments are dated from the 5th century AD.

The Dead Sea Scrolls

"In late 1946 or early 1947 a Bedouin shepherd, Muhammed edh-Dhib, followed a stray into a cave along the shores of the Dead Sea and so chanced upon the first of a group of ancient manuscripts that have since revolutionized biblical studies and the study of ancient Judaism. Seven substantial scrolls emerged from that cave, copies of biblical and extra biblical writings alike. They were only the beginning. Following the initial discovery, Bedouin and scholars competed to explore the caves of the region in hopes of new manuscript finds. After a search of hundreds of caves, eleven eventually yielded literary texts, now known as the Dead Sea Scrolls (DSS). Approximately 875 (generally fragmentary) manuscripts came to light in the course of these explorations. The nearby site of Qumran, hitherto regarded as an ancient fortress, was also excavated during five campaigns between 1952–1956, for scholars suspected that the site was connected to the caves and the scrolls.

Publication of the discoveries was comparatively rapid at first. Six of the seven major scrolls from the site of the first discovery, now known as Cave 1, were completely published within seven years.... The great bulk of the discoveries were early consigned to an international team of seven scholars from Europe and the United States. This team succeeded in sorting most of the fragments and published some of the DSS in a series of volumes, *Discoveries in the Judaean Desert* .... Five volumes of DJD appeared in the decade spanning the late 1950s and 1960s. In the decades that followed, however...the rate of publication slowed to a crawl.... The late 1980s, in particular, were marred by growing scholarly wrangling over the slow pace of publication and rights of access to the unpublished materials.

In December 1991, ... the Israel Antiquities Authority (IAA) decided to lift restrictions... Over sixty scholars were now assigned texts.... Some twenty additional volumes of DJD appeared between 1994 and early 2000." [M. O. Wise, "Dead Sea Scrolls: General Introduction", *Dictionary of New Testament Background* ed. by Evans and Porter, IVP, 2000, 252-253]

Septuagint *(See Lesson 4 for the origin of the Septuagint)*

1. The Septuagint (LXX) was the most commonly used Greek translation of the Hebrew Bible at the time of Jesus and the apostles.

2. Thus, the LXX is a translation of Hebrew manuscripts that are 1,000 years older than the MT. Not surprisingly, some of the Hebrew manuscripts in the Dead Sea Scrolls are closer to the LXX than the MT.

3. The LXX is very uneven in its quality; the Pentateuch appears to be more carefully done than the rest of the OT.

4. In a few instances, the LXX appears to reflect the original text more so than the MT, but certainty is unobtainable.

5. The *New English Translation of the Septuagint* (NETS, 2007) makes the Septuagint accessible to English readers who want to compare the LXX to the Hebrew text used by most English translations.

Samaritan Pentateuch

1. The Samaritans probably descended from the intermarriage of Israelites of the Northern Kingdom and Assyrians who were settled among them following the fall of Samaria to Assyria. Animosity existed between the Samaritans and the exiles who returned from Babylonian captivity. Ultimately, the Samaritans built their own temple on Mt. Gerizim about 400 BC.

2. "The Samaritans regard the Pentateuch alone as canonical, and they have preserved a text of these five books in Hebrew which has been transmitted independently of the Masoretic text." [Bruce, *Books*, 118]

3. Modern day Samaritans possess a scroll of the Samaritan Pentateuch which they claim was written by Abisha (1 Chr 6:4, 5, 50; Ezra 7:5), a great, grandson of Aaron. However, it is a medieval manuscript. It is written in the older, 'palaeo-Hebrew' script.

4. The Samaritan Pentateuch "has about 6,000 variations from the Masoretic text, and in nearly 2,000 of these it agrees with the Septuagint. Where the Samaritan and Septuagint texts agree against the Masoretic text, there is a *prima facie* case in favour of the former. But most of these variations are of minor significance. The most important Samaritan variants are a few which reveal the fundamental points at issue between the Samaritans and the Jews." [Bruce, *Books*, 120]

For example:

    a. In Deuteronomy 27:4-8, the MT identifies Mt. Ebal as the place where Moses commands the stones containing the Law are to be set; the Samaritan Pentateuch identifies the mountain as Mt. Gerizim.

    b. After the listing of the Ten Commandments in Exodus 20 and Deuteronomy 5, the Samaritan Pentateuch inserts a section that tells the Israelites that, when they cross the Jordan and possess the land of Canaan, they are to place the stone tablets on Mt. Gerizim and build an altar there.

5. Upon comparison of the Samaritan Pentateuch with some of the Dead Sea Scrolls, it has become apparent that the Samaritan Pentateuch is a revision of a popular Palestinian text type.

6. The Samaritan Pentateuch (or another document of which we have no knowledge) may be alluded to in Acts 7:4, 5, 32, 37 and Hebrews 9:3-4.

Aramaic Targums

1. As Hebrew was being replaced with Aramaic as the language of Palestine, it became necessary for the Hebrew Bible to be translated into Aramaic. Initially, this was accomplished by an official supplementing the reading of the Hebrew text with an oral paraphrase in Aramaic. In time, these paraphrases, called targums, were committed to writing.

2. As expected, there exists a high degree of variability between the various targums of a passage. After the fixing of the Hebrew text in about AD 100, two authoritative targums were circulated: a targum on the Pentateuch, called the Targum of Onqelos, and a Targum to the Prophets, called the Targum of Jonathan ben Uzziel.

3. There appear to be some allusions in the New Testament to the Aramaic Targums.

4. Because of the nature of the targums, their value as witnesses to the Hebrew text are limited.

Lesson 7

New Testament Text

Introduction

Even with the discovery of the Dead Sea Scrolls, the earliest extant Hebrew manuscripts of the Pentateuch were copied more than 1,000 years after the original composition of the Pentateuch. This is not uncommon with ancient writings. However, extant fragments of the New Testament writings have been found which were copied only decades after the original autograph. New Testament textual critics have an abundance of material to consider. Of course, they would still like to have more! The three main sources of information on the New Testament text are the Greek manuscripts, the ancient versions (translations) of the New Testament, and the quotations from the New Testament made by early Christians.

Greek Texts of the New Testament

The *Munster Institute for the New Testament Textual Research* maintains the list of Greek NT manuscripts. As of 2015, there were a total of 5,853 Greek manuscripts [Porter, *Fundamentals*, 50] that contain all or a part of the NT. For various reasons, there are other manuscripts of portions of the NT that are not listed [Parker, 33]. In 2002, Daniel B. Wallace formed the *Center for the Study of New Testament Manuscripts* (CSNTM) whose primary task is to digitally photograph all extant New Testament manuscripts and make them readily available.

For convenience, New Testament Greek manuscripts are classified into one of four classes on the basis of a physical characteristic (other classifications are sometimes used).

1. ***Papyri***   The oldest extant Greek manuscripts are those written on papyrus. As of 2021, 141 papyrus fragments [Wikipedia, "List of New Testament Papyri"] of the New Testament have been found (most within the last 140 years) and all were recovered from Egypt, which has the climate necessary to preserve such documents. Papyri are identified by the letter P followed by a number (P^1, P^2, ...). The following are some of the significant papyri.

a. The Chester Beatty collection (acquired by Sir Chester Beatty in 1930-1) consists of three manuscripts:

    P45 - Fragments of 30 leaves of a codex of Matthew – Acts that originally contained about 220 leaves. 3rd century document.

    P46 - 86 of the original 104 leaves of a codex containing all of Paul's epistles (except the pastorals) and Hebrews. Generally dated about AD 200, but has been dated as early as AD 100.

    P47 - 10 leaves from the middle of a codex of Revelation (9:10-17:2) that had about 32 leaves. 3rd century document.

b. The M. Martin Bodmer collection (acquired in 1955-6) consists of four manuscripts:

    P66 - Contains substantial portions of the Gospel of John. Dates from about AD 200.

    P72 - Earliest copies of Jude and the two epistles of Peter. Also contains other ancient writings. 3rd century document.

    P74 - Large codex poorly preserved that contains portions of Acts, James, 1 & 2 Peter, 1, 2, & 3 John and Jude. 7th century document.

    P75 - 102 of the original 144 pages of a codex of Luke and John. Dated between AD 175 – 225.

c. P52 – Small fragment (2.5 inches x 3.5 inches) of the Gospel of John (18:31-33, 37-38) found in 1920 (see Cover Page for picture). Dated to the first half of the second century, it has been generally agreed to be the oldest manuscript of the Greek New Testament, unless P46 or the Magdalen Papyrus can convincingly be shown to be earlier.

d. P137 – Just recently published, a small fragment of Mark (1:7-9 on one side and 1:16-18 on the other) is believed to have been copied sometime between AD 150-250.

e. The Magdalen Papyrus – Three small fragments of Matthew 26, originally dated in the 3rd to 4th century, have recently been redated by one scholar to as early as AD 70 [Thiede & D'Ancona, *Jesus Papyrus*]. This date is highly controversial and not generally accepted.

2. **Majuscules** (formerly, **Uncials**)   In antiquity, Greek literary works were written in a formal style called *majuscule* or *uncial*. Although our Greek papyri manuscripts are written in this style, the class of manuscripts called *majuscules* refers to *parchment* manuscripts. Parchment was more expensive than papyrus and, thus, does not seem to have been used by Christians until Constantine favored Christianity in the 4th century. In fact, Constantine ordered 50 copies of the Old and New Testaments be prepared. Initially, majuscules were identified by letters (A, B, C, etc.), but as the number of majuscule manuscripts increased,

they are now identified with a two or more-digit number. There are 323 extant majuscules [Porter, *Fundamentals*, 50].

a. *Codex Sinaiticus* (01, Aleph) – Dated to AD 350 and found in a monastery at Mt. Sinai, this is a large codex originally containing the Old Testament (Septuagint), New Testament, and other Christian writings. Parts of the Old Testament have perished, but all of the New Testament remains; it is the only majuscule to contain the entire New Testament.

b. *Codex Alexandrinus* (02, A) – 5th century manuscript contains most of the Old Testament and New Testament.

c. *Codex Vaticanus* (03, B) – Dated to about AD 350, this codex is considered by many to be the most important majuscule. Much of Hebrews and all of 1 & 2 Timothy, Titus, Philemon, and Revelation are missing. Because of their date, many have suggested that Codex Sinaiticus and Codex Vaticanus were among the 50 copies prepared for Constantine. This is by no means certain.

d. *Codex Ephraemi* (04, C) – This manuscript is a palimpsest ('re-scraped'), which is a document that has had the original writing 'erased' and now contains newer writing. There are 55 majuscule palimpsests. The original writing of Codex Ephraemi was a 5th century Greek manuscript of the Old and New Testaments. This was erased and overwritten in the 12th century with sermons of St. Ephreaem. Only a small portion of the Old Testament and about 5/8th of the New Testament remains.

e. *Codex Bezae* (05, D) – 5th or 6th century manuscript that has Greek text on the left page and the corresponding Latin text on the right page. Only the Gospels, Acts, and a small fragment of 3 John is extant.

3. **Minuscules**   About the 9th century, a modified cursive Greek script called *minuscule* was commonly adopted. The use of this script enabled manuscripts to be produced at a greater rate. That and the fact that these manuscripts are more recent (hence, less likely to have been lost) means that we have many more minuscules than majuscules. As of 2015, there are 2,931 minuscules [Porter, *Fundamentals*, 50]. Minuscules are identified by a number. Codex 33 is a minuscule manuscript of the entire New Testament (except Revelation) and is very similar in its text to Aleph and B. The vast majority of minuscules are on parchment, but a few later manuscripts are on paper.

4. **Lectionaries**   "Very early in the Christian era certain sections of the New Testament were selected for reading in services on each day of the year. Some New Testament manuscripts have indications in their margins of the beginnings and endings of these sections. Before long, however, these passages were assembled in the order in which they were to be read, and were copied in that order in manuscripts called 'lectionaries,' or lesson books" [Greenlee, 28-29]. As of 2015, there are 2,465 lectionaries [Porter, *Fundamentals*, 50]; about 10 percent are majuscules and 90 percent are minuscules. Most are from the 8th century or later.

The Codex Sinaiticus

"Arguably the most important person to discover, identify, and publish NT manuscripts is the German scholar from Leipzig, Constantine Tischendorf. Living in the nineteenth century, Tischendorf devoted his career as a scholar to discovering and publishing as many Greek NT (as well as other biblical and other language) manuscripts as he could find, so that he could establish the early reliability of the NT text. He undertook this task in direct opposition to the rise of German higher criticism, which was increasingly skeptical of the reliability of the NT. In the course of his travels to various places around Europe and the Middle East, Tischendorf discovered, identified, and published more manuscripts than any other scholar in history before or since. ...

The most important of them all, however, was his discovery of Codex Sinaiticus (01 א), which he identified in St. Catherine's Monastery at the base of Mount Sinai in the Sinai Peninsula. Tischendorf visited St. Catherine's Monastery three times. On the first trip, in 1844, he found the monks burning what he identified as the earliest manuscript he had ever seen — apparently they were cold and needed fodder for their fire! He was able to save the manuscript and was given a number of pages of the OT in Greek, which he took back to Leipzig and published. After a second trip, in 1853, during which it appeared that the manuscript had been forgotten or had disappeared, Tischendorf revisited the monastery one last time in 1859, and was shown the remains of the manuscript first seen in 1844. Through a process of negotiation, Tischendorf was able to borrow the manuscript so that it could first be copied, and then published, in 1862 in a beautiful facsimile edition sponsored by the czar of Russia. For this beautiful edition, of which only three hundred twenty-seven copies of the four-volume edition were printed, Tischendorf found special paper and designed a unique font, which included several different types of various characters so as to capture the original as realistically as possible. There is some controversy over how the manuscript came to be given to the czar, but the evidence is that the monks at the time bequeathed the manuscript to the czar in return for a number of considerations. This manuscript was later sold by the Soviet government in 1933 to the British people for £100,000, and it can be viewed today in the British Library." [Porter and Pitts, *Fundamentals of New Testament Textual Criticism*, 56-57].

Versions and Patristic Quotations

The Greek New Testament was soon translated into other languages such as Syriac (2nd/3rd century), Latin (2nd century), Coptic (3rd century), Gothic (4th century), Armenian (5th century), Georgian (?), Ethiopic (4th to 7th century), Old Slavonic (9th century), etc. One of the most important versions and the version with the most extant copies (8,000) is the Latin Vulgate prepared by Jerome about 400. Commissioned by Pope Damascus, an updated Vulgate, the New Vulgate, is still used by the Roman Catholic Church. The next most prevalent extant version is the Armenian version with over 1,200 extant copies. It is considered one of the most reliable versions.

The usefulness of the versions as witnesses to the Greek text is complicated by many factors: the inability of any second language to completely convey the form and meaning of the original language; the uncertainty which Greek text or texts were used for the basis of the translations; the corruption and variability among the extant copies of the version; etc. Most importantly, a version can testify to the existence of any given phrase in the Greek text used for the version.

Patristic (from Latin *'father'*) writings of the early centuries are filled with quotations of New Testament writings (and the Old Testament also). "So extensive are these citations that if all other sources for our knowledge of the text of the New Testament were destroyed, they would be sufficient alone for the reconstruction of practically the entire New Testament" [Metzger, *NT Text*, 86]. The most important use of patristic quotations is to ascertain the time and place certain Greek texts were used which help to determine the history and transmission of various Greek text types. However, our extant copies of the writings of the early Christians are also the result of a copying process.

The Printed Greek Text

The invention of the printing press by Gutenberg in the 15th century ultimately brought to an end the hand copying of manuscripts; some manuscripts from the 16th century exist. The first Bibles to be printed in 1456 were the Latin Vulgate; about 40 copies of this edition, the Gutenberg Bible, are in existence today. The first Greek New Testament to be printed and distributed to the public was prepared by Erasmus and placed on sale in 1516 (although another Greek New Testament by Cardinal Ximenes had been printed in 1514, but was not placed on the market until 1522 when the Old Testament printing was completed and both had been approved by the Pope). Erasmus only had about six Greek manuscripts of the New Testament, not one of which contained the complete New Testament. Erasmus' text, with some revisions, became in essence the "Received Text" (*Textus Receptus*) that was the basis of early English versions, including the *King James Version*.

New Testament Textual Criticism

The task of the New Testament textual critic is to determine the original wording of the Greek New Testament. By understanding the nature of errors that can occur in hand copying (to be studied in the next lesson), the textual critic makes judgments as to the original wording.

It has also been important to understand the literary history of a text. Textual critics are generally agreed that there are three major text types, or families of texts, based on the characteristics that the extant manuscripts display. These text types are:

Alexandrian – Text type generally believed to best represent the original text. It is widely thought that skilled editors trained in the scholarly traditions of Alexandria prepared this text. The oldest manuscripts belong to this family, e.g., P66, P75, Aleph, B, C, L.

Western – The text type that circulated widely in the west (North Africa, Italy, Gaul), but also in Egypt and other eastern areas. The Western text type can be traced to early dates, but is generally considered not to be as reliable as the Alexandrian text type. Represented by Codex D and Old Latin manuscripts.

Byzantine – Text type that may have originated in Antioch and taken to Constantinople. Became the standard text type of the Greek Orthodox Church. As Greek was being replaced by Latin as the language in the West, the vast majority of Greek manuscripts produced after the 6th century were of the Byzantine text type. Consequently, over 80 percent of all manuscripts are of this text type [Wegner, *Textual Criticism*, 244]. The Byzantine text type is the basis of the Textus Receptus.

Textual scholars used to identify another text type called **Caesarean** that was believed to be associated with Origen in Caesarea, which he may have brought from Egypt (Alexandria). It is now seen as a mixture of Western and Alexandrian readings (Porter, *How We Got*, 61).

In evaluating the various readings, textual critics use the following basic criteria; of course, there are exceptions to all these guidelines [Metzger, *NT Text*, 209-210]:

I. External Evidence

    A. The date of the manuscripts. In general, earlier manuscripts are to be preferred.

    B. The geographical distribution of manuscripts that agree in supporting a variant. A variant supported by independent, but widely distributed, manuscripts receives greater weight.

    C. The text family to which the manuscript belongs. "Evidence is to be weighed, not counted."

II. Internal Evidence

    A. Transcriptional Probabilities (concerns the transmission process)
       1. Which reading best explains the others.
       2. In general, the more difficult reading is to be preferred.
       3. In general, the shorter reading is to be preferred.
       4. Possibility that scribes tried to harmonize divergent passages.
       5. Possibility that unfamiliar word replaced with more familiar or less refined grammar improved.

    B. Intrinsic Probabilities (concerns the author)
       1. The style and vocabulary of the author throughout the book.
       2. The immediate context.
       3. Harmony with the usage of the author elsewhere.

At present, the two critical Greek texts commonly used are *The Greek New Testament* [5th Edition, 2014] published by the United Bible Society and the Nestle-Aland *Novum Testamentum Graece* [28th Edition, 2012]. The same Greek text is used for both. These texts are sometimes called eclectic texts which means that no single ancient text was used as the basis, but the text at each point was determined by applying the criteria stated above. This tends to emphasize the internal evidence over the external. Two of the more influential earlier textual critics, B.F. Westcott and F.J.A. Hort, gave preference to the external evidence, i.e., to the earlier documents. Thus, their Greek text is based almost solely on texts of the Alexandrian text type family. (Westcott and Hort's text was used as the basis for the *Revised Version* of 1881 and the *American Standard Version* of 1901.)

Although the vast majority of scholars agree that the standard eclectic texts best represent the original autographs, some scholars argue for the supremacy of the Byzantine text type believing that the wide attestation of the Byzantine text type is not by accident, but rather due to divine providence [e.g., Sturz, 32f]. Thus, a modern critical text, called the Majority text, has been prepared based on the readings that occur most. Although the Majority text is not identical to the Textus Receptus, it is very close. Generally, those who argue for the superiority of the Byzantine text type also argue for the superiority of the King James Version.

Ancient Texts

"The evidence for our New Testament writings is ever so much greater than the evidence for many writings of classical authors, the authenticity of which no-one dreams of questioning. ... It is a curious fact that historians have often been much readier to trust the New Testament records than have many theologians. ...

Perhaps we can appreciate how wealthy the New Testament is in manuscript attestation if we compare the textual material for other ancient historical works. For Caesar's *Gallic War* (composed between 58 and 50 BC) there are several extant MSS, but only nine or ten are good, and the oldest is some 900 years later than Caesar's day. Of the 142 books of the Roman History of Livy (59 BC-AD 17) only thirty-five survive; these are known to us from not more than twenty MSS of any consequence, only one of which, and that containing fragments of Books iii-vi, is as old as the fourth century. Of the fourteen books of the *Histories* of Tacitus (*c.* AD 100) only four and a half survive; of the sixteen books of his *Annals,* ten survive in full and two in part. The text of these extant portions of his two great historical works depends entirely on two MSS, one of the ninth century and one of the eleventh. The extant MSS of his minor works *(Dialogus de Oratoribus, Agricola, Germania)* all descend from a codex of the tenth century. The History of Thucydides (*c.* 460-400 BC) is known to us from eight MSS, the earliest belonging to *c.* AD 900, and a few papyrus scraps, belonging to about the beginning of the Christian era. The same is true of the History of Herodotus (*c.* 480-425 BC). Yet no classical scholar would listen to an argument that the authenticity of Herodotus or Thucydides is in doubt because the earliest MSS of their works which are of any use to us are over 1,300 years later than the originals." [F.F. Bruce, *The New Testament Documents*, 15-16]

Lesson 8

Nature and Types of Errors in Transmission

Introduction

Scribes manually copying manuscripts would inevitability make mistakes and it is important to understand the type of errors that arose during transmission so that the original text can be reliably reconstructed. The majority of this lesson's material is derived from Metzger, *The Text of the New Testament*, Chapter VII, and concerns errors other than those that may have arisen due to *scripto continua* (see Lesson 3).

Unintentional Changes

Scribal practices varied in copying the Biblical manuscripts. Sometimes a scribe would work in solitude, carefully reading the "parent" manuscript (called the exemplar) and then writing the new manuscript. At other times, scribes worked together with one reading the exemplar and several scribes then writing new manuscripts according to what they heard. Each scenario gave rise to its own particular set of unintentional errors.

1. ### *Misreads of Manuscripts*

   The first two misreads would only occur with majuscule manuscripts.

   a. 2 Peter 2:18 ΟΛΙΓΟΣ "scarcely" → "*just escaped*" (NRSV)
      ΟΝΤΟΣ "really" → "*clean escaped*" (KJV)
      "*actually escaped*" (NKJV)

   b. 1 Timothy 3:16 ΟΣ "he who" → "*He was revealed in the flesh*" (NRSV)
      ΘΣ "God" → "*God was manifest in the flesh*" (KJV)

   A characteristic of New Testament manuscripts is the use of contractions for various sacred words; especially the names of God. For God, Jesus, Christ, Lord, etc. the contraction would be formed by only writing the first and last characters of the name and, then, to indicate that it is a contraction a horizontal bar would be placed over the two letters.

c. 1 Corinthians 13:3   καυτησο☐αι   *"surrender my body to the flames"* (NIV, earlier eds.)

καυχησωαι   *"hand over my body that I may boast"* (NRSV, NIV, NET, NASB (2020))

d. Errors due to a *homoioteletuon* (a similar ending of lines)

1 John 2:23 "No one who denies the Son has the Father; everyone who confesses the Son has the Father also" (NRSV). The repetition of the phrase *"has the Father"* apparently caused one or more scribes to mistakenly omit the entire second phrase (*"everyone…also"*) which does not occur in later manuscripts (see KJV).

John 17:15 "I pray not that thou shouldest take them from the [world, but that thou shouldest keep them from the] evil one" (ASV). The repetition of *"from the"* undoubtedly confused the scribe of the Codex Vaticanus, which omits the bracketed words. The resulting text must have given much puzzlement to its readers!

e. Errors due to a *dittography* (a letter or word written twice instead of once)

Acts 27:37 *"We were in all two hundred seventy-six persons in the ship."* The Codex Vaticanus reads *"about seventy-six"*.

ΕΝΤΩΠΛΟΙΩΣΟΣ   (in the ship) *"two hundred seventy-six"* (KJV, ESV)

ΕΝΤΩΠΛΟΙΩΩΣΟΣ   (in the ship) *"about seventy-six"*

2. *Similar Sounding Words Mistaken (homophony)* [e.g., the English homonyms *great* and *grate*]

a. Romans 5:1   εχο☐εν☐ *"we have"* (NAU; NRSV, REB)
            εχω☐εν   *"let us"* (NEB)

b. Revelation 1:5   λουσαντι *"and washed us from our sins"* (KJV)
            λυσαντι   *"and freed us from our sins"* (NRSV)

c. 1 John 1:4   υ☐ων☐ *"that your joy may be full"* (KJV)
            η☐ων   *"that our joy may be complete"* (NRSV)

These similar sounding words are also similar in form, so the differences could have resulted from being misread.

3. **Errors of Judgment**   At times scribes had to make a judgment about the text they were copying. This is especially true of marginal notes. Corrections to a text were sometimes placed in the margin, but scribes would also add notes regarding the text in the margin. A subsequent scribe would have to discern the nature of the marginal note.

   a. John 5:3-4   Verses 3b-4 ("*waiting for the moving of the water. For an angel went down at a certain season into the pool and stirred up the water: whoever then first after the stirring of the water stepped in was made well of whatsoever disease he had.*" KJV) are omitted in earlier texts, and consequently omitted in modern English versions, e.g., ESV. Probably a marginal note explaining the water movement that later was interpreted by a scribe as a textual correction.

Intentional Changes

Some changes appear to be intentional on the part of the scribe. A scribe in good faith may have thought that a corruption existed in the text that needed correcting. Or, a scribe may have made a change due to a doctrinal consideration; either, to "improve" the acceptability of a text or to make a text support a favored belief or practice. From the early centuries of Christianity, Christians have accused others and have been accused by others of changing the text of Scripture.

1. **Addition of Natural Complements**   These may have been unintentional errors of the mind, but it is also easy to see them as intentional. The general presumption by most textural critics is that the shorter reading is the original.

   a. Matthew 26:3   "*chief priests and the elders*" (NRSV)
      "*chief priests, and the scribes, and the elders*" (KJV)

   b. Matthew 6:4, 6   "*and your Father who sees in secret will reward you*" (NRSV)
      "*...shall reward thee openly*" (KJV)

   c. 1 Corinthians 7:5   "*prayer*" (NRSV)
      "*prayer and fasting*" (KJV).

      This addition may have been added by monks who emphasized asceticism. (See also Mk 9:29 and Acts 10:30)

   d. Galatians 6:17   "*for I carry the marks of Jesus*" (NRSV)
      "*...the Lord Jesus*" (KJV)
      "*...the Lord Jesus Christ*" (Some manuscripts)
      "*...our Lord Jesus Christ*" (Some manuscripts)

2. **Harmonistic Changes** In the Gospels especially there seems to be the efforts of some scribes to harmonize the four Gospel accounts. This tendency also occurred sometimes in the quotation of Old Testament Scriptures. Again, some of these could be unintentional errors of the mind.

   a. Matthew 19:17   *"Why do you ask me about what is good? There is only one who is good."* (NRSV)

      "...there is none good but one, that is, God" (KJV). This form agrees with Mark 10:17 and Luke 18:18.

   b. Luke 11:2-4   In some manuscripts, the shorter form of the Lord's Prayer in Luke is enlarged to agree with Matthew 6.

   c. Matthew 15:8 *"This people draweth nigh unto me with their mouth, and honoureth me with their lips..."* (KJV). The phrase *"draweth ... and"* is not in earlier manuscripts, but it is found in Isaiah 29:13.

3. **Refinements**

   a. Mark 1:2   *"As it is written in the prophet Isaiah..."* (NRSV)

      "As it is written in the prophets..." (KJV)

      Since the citation is actually a combination of Malachi 3:1 and Isaiah 40:3, did a scribe think he was correcting an earlier mistake? Or, maybe, just making the text a little better?

   b. 1 Corinthians 11:29   *"all who eat and drink"* (NRSV)

      "he that eateth and drinketh unworthily" (KJV).

      Did a scribe add *"unworthily"* in v.29 because of its presence in v.27 and thus was making doubly sure that the point was understood? Or, should this be considered an unintentional mental repetition?

4. **Conflation**   It appears that if a decision could not be made as to which was original, then both were included; typical of the Byzantine text type.

   a. Luke 24:53   *"blessing God"* (NRSV)
      "praising God" (Some manuscripts) Why might this happen?
      "praising and blessing God" (KJV)

   b. Mark 13:11   *"do not worry beforehand about what you are to say"* (NRSV)
      "do not premeditate (or practice) beforehand" (Some manuscripts)
      "do not worry beforehand, or premeditate what you shall speak" (NKJV)

5. **Bias**

   a. The reviser of the Bezan text "shows his dislike to the prominence assigned to women in Acts." Thus, [Ramsay, *St. Paul the Traveller and Roman Citizen*, 268]

      1. Aquila is listed before Priscilla.
      2. In 17:12, changes "not a few of the honourable Greek women and of men" to "of the Greeks and the honourable many men and women."
      3. In 17:34, omits Damaris.
      4. In 17:4, changes "leading women" into "wives of leading men."

6. **Doctrinal Correctness**

   a. Luke 23:32   *"And also other criminals, two, were led away with him to be crucified"* (Early manuscripts P75, ℵ, B).

      "There were also two others, criminals, led with Him to be put to death" (NKJV, NRSV sim.).

      Presumably, scribes wanted to make it clear that Jesus was not a criminal.

   b. Matthew 24:36   *"But of that day and hour no one knows, neither the angels in heaven, nor the Son, but only the Father"* (NRSV).

      "nor the Son" is omitted (KJV).

      Did the scribe copying Matthew disagree with the idea that Jesus, as Deity, did not know something? [Or is this a case of harmonizing where the phrase *"nor the Son"* was *added* to harmonize with Mark 13:32?]

What Does All This Mean?

One might easily get the impression that our Scriptures are filled with errors. Unfortunately, some try to reinforce this impression. But that conclusion is unwarranted.

"Bruce K. Waltke notes that in the *Biblia Hebraica Stuttgartensia* (the most recent critical edition of the Hebrew Bible; ...) approximately one textual note appears for every ten words; thus, 90 percent of the text is without significant variation. According to Shemaryahu Talmon, even the errors and textural variations that exist 'affect the intrinsic message only in relatively few instances.' Similarly, in the New Testament, the fourth edition of the United Bible Societies ... *Greek New Testament* text notes variants regarding approximately 500 out of 6,900 words, or only about seven percent of the text. Textual criticism, therefore, mainly concerns itself with this small portion of the biblical text called 'variant readings.' A variant reading is any difference in wording (e.g., differences in spelling, added or omitted words) that occurs among manuscripts." [Wegner, *Textual Criticism*, 24-25]

Lesson 9

The Bible in Translation

Introduction

For God's word to be powerful it must, at the very least, be *preached* to people in their native language, but it is far better if people can *read* it in their native language. This has not always been the case; even today the Bible has still not been translated into some languages. For English-speaking people, there are a host of translations to choose from today. This lesson surveys the history of Bible translation, with an emphasis on English Translations.

Septuagint

Recalling Lesson 4 and 6, the Old Testament was translated into Greek about 200 years before the writing of the New Testament books. It was widely used and respected. The notable preference of New Testament writers to frequently cite the Septuagint (LXX) instead of the Hebrew Bible underscores the notion that God's word can be just as trustworthy in the form of a translation as it is in the original language. This point is especially significant given the variations between the LXX and the Hebrew Bible.

Latin Vulgate

Latin was the language of Ancient Rome and, although Greek initially was the universal language as Rome took over the former Greek Empire of Alexander, was the language of commerce and government until the Renaissance. The earliest surviving Latin manuscripts are from the early 3rd Century, but the Latin translation undertaken by Jerome from about AD 383 to 405 became the dominant translation for nearly 1,000 years. It was called the Vulgate because it was written in the common (or, *vulgar*) language of the people.

Jerome was commissioned to produce this translation by Pope Damascus to replace the multitude of conflicting Latin translations then in use. Jerome fully understood that he was placed in a "no-win" situation since many had become comfortable with their translations and would, no doubt, become outraged at his. Jerome was right and he was often attacked, especially for his decision to translate the Old Testament directly from Hebrew manuscripts instead of using the Septuagint.

It was not until the 9th century that the Vulgate was firmly established as the preeminent translation. Other Latin translations were produced, but in 1546 the Council of Trent formally declared the Vulgate to be the official Bible of the Roman Catholic Church. It was revised and replaced as the "Authorized Version" in 1592 with the Clementine Vulgate (produced during the reign of Pope Clement VIII).

Early Ancient Versions

Although the Latin versions, and especially the Vulgate, were the most influential in early Christianity, there were many people who were unable to read Latin and thus in need of a translation in their native language. Two of the earliest and most influential were the Syriac and Coptic versions.

Syriac Perhaps the earliest translation of the New Testament was into the Syriac language. Antioch of Syria was the third largest city in the Roman Empire and as the Gospel was spread in the surrounding areas of Syria the need became apparent for a rendition of the New Testament into Syriac. At least parts of the New Testament begin to circulate in Syriac at the end of the second century or beginning of the third. Only two manuscripts of this early version that only contain the Gospels have survived. Various Syriac versions have existed, but the form that has prevailed is called the Peshitta. It is still used by Syriac-speaking churches.

Coptic The ancient Egyptian language was written in hieroglyphs. But due to its difficulty, a new (and last) form called Coptic was developed in the first and early second century that adopted the 24 letters of the Greek alphabet and supplemented them with seven characters from demotic [Porter, *How We Got*, 157]. Coptic developed with the spread of Christianity. Coptic translations of the New Testament arose in the third and fourth centuries. Although the Coptic language ceased being used by the 17th century, it remains the ecclesiastical language of the Coptic Church. Coptic existed in differing dialects (Sahidic being the oldest, but Bohairic becoming the predominant), but all used the Septuagint as the basis for the Old Testament and the text used for the New Testament falls within the Alexandrian family of texts.

Early English Versions

The earliest English versions were translations of the Vulgate. Although we know that Christianity was taken to Britain by the early 4th century, the first complete translation was not produced until the period of Middle English (a mixture of Norman and English) with the translations of John Wycliffe (1329-84; there are two translations associated with Wycliffe and it is unknown whether he actually translated portions of either). Previous to this there were only portions of Scriptures translated in Old English by Aldhelm, Bede, Alfred the Great, etc.

Wycliffe disagreed with many of the teachings of the Roman Catholic Church and felt that the Church's errors would become widely known if people had the ability to read the Scriptures in their own language. Consequently, the Roman Catholic Church called Wycliffe a heretic and, although he died a natural death, decades later his bones were dug up, burned, and their ashes scattered in a river. Englishmen caught reading Wycliffe's version were subject to having their possessions confiscated. John Huss, Wycliffe's follower, was burned at the stake.

The Reformation created a great deal of unrest in Europe. In part this was fueled by Luther's translation of the Scriptures into German in 1522. In 1526, William Tyndale printed an English New Testament based on Greek manuscripts. Portions of the Old Testament were completed by 1530 and a second edition of his New Testament was published in 1534. Tyndale could not get ecclesiastical authority to produce his translation, thus he had to leave England to do his work. Tyndale's motivation was also to provide his countryman direct access to God's teachings. He is quoted as telling a clergyman, "If God spare my life, ere many years, I will cause a boy that driveth the plough to know more of the Scripture than thou dost." Ultimately, he was denounced as a heretic and burned at the stake on October 6, 1536.

Two associates of Tyndale, Miles Coverdale and John Rogers, produced English translations. The Coverdale Bible, published in 1535 outside of Britain, was based primarily on Tyndale's translation with comparison made to Latin and German versions. It was the first complete *printed* Bible in English and, following Jerome, it was the first to separate the books of the Apocrypha from the other Old Testament books. In 1537, John Rogers produced a version called Matthew's Bible that was based on both Tyndale's and Coverdale's versions. That same year, the Coverdale Bible and the Matthew Bible received license from King Henry VIII for distribution within England. Also in 1537, Coverdale revised Matthew's Bible to produce the version called the Great Bible, which King Henry VIII had placed in every church in England. Rogers was later martyred during the reign of Queen Mary.

Two competing translations were produced during the reign of Queen Elizabeth. The *Geneva Bible*, completed in Geneva in 1560, was a revision of the *Great Bible* (Old Testament) and *Matthew's Bible* (New Testament). It was a superior translation, but its marginal notes were heavily Reformed (Calvinistic), which were not well received by the Anglican bishops. Thus, the bishops revised the *Great Bible* and produced the *Bishop's Bible* in 1568. Queen Elizabeth made it the authorized version to be placed in all the churches of England.

King James Version

By the time of King James I (reign from 1604-25), literary scholarship had made great strides in England (e.g., Shakespeare, Spenser, Bacon, Johnson, etc.). James himself was well-educated. Upon his ascension to the throne, Puritans made an appeal on several matters. For the most part, James refused to grant the Puritans wishes, except that he did agree to a new translation. The translation was to be based on the original Hebrew (Masoretic Text) and Greek (*Textus Receptus*, "Received Text") Scriptures and no marginal notes were to be included. He hoped this would bring unity to all the English people. Although the *Geneva Bible* still remained popular for some time, the *King James Version*, completed in 1611, became the Bible *par excellence* for all English-speaking people for over 300 years. Its phraseology is indebted to all the earlier English translations, but especially to William Tyndale.

After the King James Version

English, like all living languages, evolves and changes with time. Words, once clearly understood, become archaic. To get a sense of how English has changed over time, compare the following three early English versions of the Lord's Prayer in Luke 11:2b-4:

Wycliffite (Wycliffe) Bible (c.1384)
[http://wesley.nnu.edu/biblical_studies/wycliffe/Luk.txt]

> Fadir, halewid be thi name. Thi kyngdom come to. Yyue `to vs to dai oure ech daies breed. And foryyue to vs oure synnes, as we foryyuen to ech man that owith to vs. And lede vs not in to temptacioun.

Tyndale New Testament (1525) [Jeffrey, *Dictionary of Biblical Tradition*, 878]

> Oure father which arte in heve, hallowed be thy name. Lett thy kyngdo come. They will be fulfilet, even in erth as it is in heven. Oure dayly bred geve us this daye. And forgeve us oure synnes: For even we forgeve every man that traspasseth us; and ledde us not into temptacio, Butt deliver vs from evyll Amen.

King James Bible (1611) [Jeffrey, *Dictionary of Biblical Tradition*, 878]

> Our Father which art in heauen, Halowed be thy Name, Thy kingdome come, Thy will be done as in heauen, so in earth. Giue vs day by day our dayly bread. And forgiue vs our sinnes: for wee also forgiue euery one that is indebted to vs. And lead vs not into temptation, but deliuer vs from euill.

Thus, it was inevitable that the *King James Version* would require revision to continue to be understandable. The current standard text of the KJV is based on the 1769 Oxford edition. The primary focus of at least four current translations (*King James II*, *New Kings James Version*, *21st Century King James Version,* and *Modern English Version*) has simply been to update the language of the *King James Version*.

Yet there are other advances in knowledge that have been used by some translators. Our understanding of Hebrew vocabulary is constantly growing as other documents in Hebrew and its sister languages are found. With regard to the New Testament, the great number of Greek texts now available to the translator increases our understanding of the text, thereby providing a better base from which to begin. Most modern translations take advantage of this growth in textual knowledge.

A Tribute to the King James Version

"The two greatest influences on the shaping of the English language are the works of William Shakespeare and the English translation that appeared in 1611. The King James Bible – named for the King of England who ordered the production of a fresh translation in 1604 – is both a religious and literary classic. Literary scholars have heaped praise upon it. Nineteenth-century writers and literary critics acclaimed it as the 'noblest monument of English prose.' In a series of lectures at Cambridge University during the First World War, Sir Arthur Quiller-Couch declared that the King James Bible was 'the very greatest' literary achievement in the English language. The only possible challenger for this title came from the complete works of Shakespeare. His audience had no quarrel with this judgment. It was the accepted wisdom of the age.

"The King James Bible was a landmark in the history of the English language, and an inspiration to poets, dramatists, artists, and politicians. The influence of this work has been incalculable. For many years, it was the only English translation of the Bible available. Many families could afford only one book – a Bible, in whose pages parents recorded the births of their children, and found solace at their deaths. Countless youngsters learned to read by mouthing the words they found in the only book the family possessed – the King James Bible. Many learned passages by heart, and found that their written and spoken English was shaped by the language and imagery of this Bible. Without the King James Bible, there would have been no *Paradise Lost*, no *Pilgrim's Progress*, no Handel's *Messiah*, no Negro spirituals, and no Gettysburg Address. These, and innumerable other works, were inspired by the language of this Bible. Without this Bible, the culture of the English-speaking world would have been immeasurably impoverished. The King James Bible played no small part in shaping English literary nationalism, by asserting the supremacy of the English language as a means of conveying religious truths.

... "Throughout the sixteenth and seventeenth centuries, the Bible was seen as a social, economic, and political text. Those seeking to overthrow the English monarchy and those wanting to retain it both sought support from the same Bible. The Bible came to be seen as the foundation of every aspect of English culture, linking monarch and church, time and eternity.

"The lives of countless men and women since then have been changed and molded by the King James Bible. Refugees from England, fleeing religious persecution in the seventeenth century, brought copies with them. It would be their encouragement on the long and dangerous voyage to the Americas, and their guide as they settled in the New World. Prisoners in English jails found solace in reciting biblical verses they had learned by heart, in the words of the translators assembled by King James. The King James Bible became part of the everyday world of generations of English-speaking peoples, spread across the world. It can be argued that, until the end of the First World War, the King James Bible was seen, not simply as the most important English translation of the Bible, but as one of the finest literary works in the English language. It did

The King James Version Family Tree

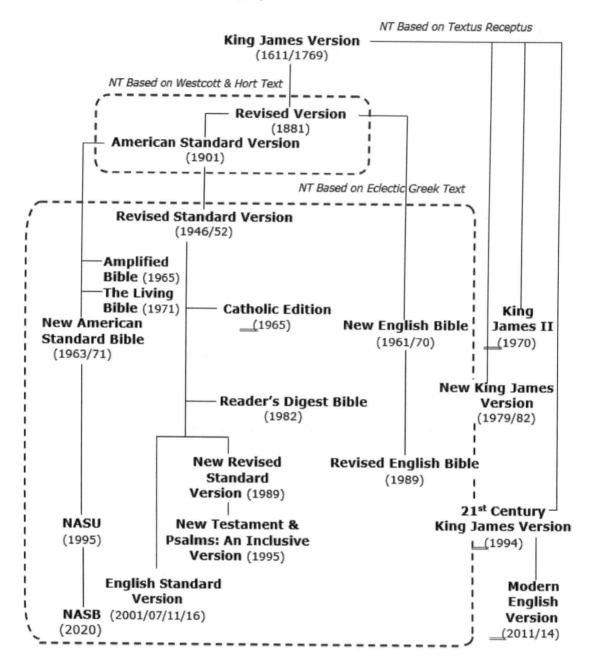

Roman Catholic English Bibles

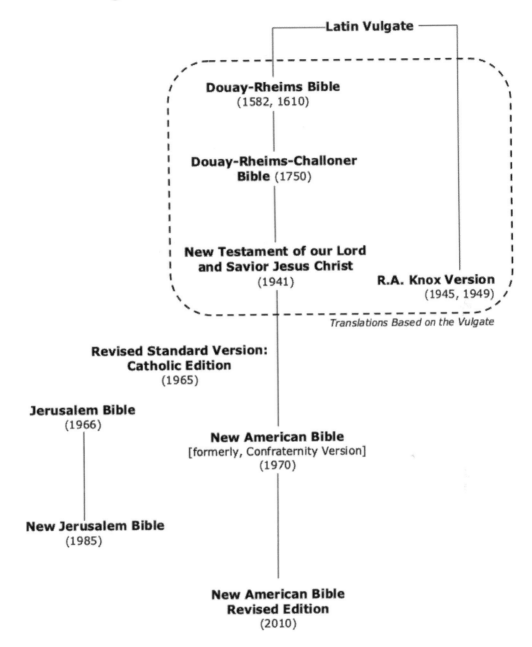

Latin Vulgate

Douay-Rheims Bible
(1582, 1610)

**Douay-Rheims-Challoner
Bible** (1750)

**New Testament of our Lord
and Savior Jesus Christ**
(1941)

R.A. Knox Version
(1945, 1949)

Translations Based on the Vulgate

**Revised Standard Version:
Catholic Edition**
(1965)

Jerusalem Bible
(1966)

New American Bible
[formerly, Confraternity Version]
(1970)

New Jerusalem Bible
(1985)

**New American Bible
Revised Edition**
(2010)

Current and Recent English Translations

AB	*Amplified Bible* (1965)
ASV	*American Standard Version* (1901)
AT	*The Bible: An American Translation* (Goodspeed, 1923/31; Revised 1935)
Barclay	*Barclay's New Testament* (1969)
BLE	*Bible in Living English* (Byington, 1972)
CEB	*Common English Bible* (NT 2010; OT/Apoc 2011)
CEV	*Contemporary English Version* (1995)
CSB	*Christian Standard Bible* (NT 1999/OT 2004/2009; 2017)
ESV	*English Standard Version* (2001/07/11/16)
GW	*God's Word* (1995)
GNT	*Good News Translation* (formerly *Good News for Modern Man* or *Today's English Version* (1966/76/GNT 2001)
IEB	*International English Bible* (2014)
JB	*Jerusalem Bible* (1966)
KJV	*King James Version* (1611/1769)
KJ21	*21st Century King James Version* (Gary, 1994)
LB	*The Living Bible* (Taylor, 1967/71; a paraphrase of ASV)
LEV	*Literal English Version* – based on WEB (2016)
LSV	*Literal Standard Version* – based on Young's Literal (2020)
MEV	*Modern English Version* (NT 2011/OT 2014)
Moffatt	*A New Translation* (Moffatt, 1913/26; Revised 1935)
Msg	*The Message* (Peterson,1993/2002)
MLB	*Modern Language Bible* (Verkuyl, 1945/1959; Berkeley)
NAB	*New American Bible* (1970)
NABRE	*New American Bible, Revised Ed.* (2010)
NET	*The NET Bible* (*New English Translation*) (2005, 1st Edition; 2019)
NASB	*New American Standard Bible* (NT 1963/OT 1971; Updated 1995, 2020)
NCV	*New Century Version* (1991; International Children's Bible)
NEB	*New English Bible* (1961/1970)
NIV	*New International Version* (NT 1973/OT 78/84/2005/11)
NIrV	*New International Readers Version* (1995)
NJB	*New Jerusalem Bible* (1985; Revision of JB)
NJV	*New Jewish Version* (1985)
NKJV	*New King James Version* (NT 1979/OT 1982)
NLT	*New Living Translation* (1996/2004; Revision of The Living Bible)

Growth of Translations

NRSV	*New Revised Standard Version* (1989; Revision of RSV)
NTPI	*New Testament and Psalms: An Inclusive Version* (1995)
NWT	*New World Translation of the Holy Scriptures* (1950/1961; Revised 1981)
Phillips	*New Testament in Modern English* (1958; Revised 1972)
RDB	*Reader's Digest Bible* (1982)
REB	*Revised English Bible* (1989; Revision of NEB)
RSV	*Revised Standard Version* (NT 1946/OT 1952)
RV	*Revised Version* (1881/85)
WEB	*World English Bible* – updated version of ASV (2014, 2022)
Williams	*New Testament: A Translation in the Language of the People* (1937)

Note: *If the translation was by an individual, that individual's name is given first in the parenthesis. The date given is the date of publication; if two dates are given, the first date is publication date for the New Testament and the second date for the Old Testament.*

Lesson 10

Translation Issues (I)

Introduction

Before translating can commence, Bible translators must first make several decisions regarding the nature of their translation. Each of these decisions will impact the usefulness and reliability of the resulting translation. Readers selecting a translation should understand the issues at stake and how each translation approaches these issues. The following issues will be the focus of the next three lessons:

- Translators: Number, Qualifications, and Bias
- Target Reader
- Text Selection
- Type of Translation: Verbal, Dynamic, or Free
- Translation Format
- Names and Pronouns for God
- Gender
- Units and Measures

Translators: Number, Qualifications, and Bias

To adequately translate the entire Bible, an excellent knowledge of Hebrew (& Aramaic) and Greek is required. Since few individuals have a thorough knowledge of both, most individual translations have been of the New Testament (e.g., Weymouth, Goodspeed, Williams, Barclay, Phillips, et.al.). Those individuals who have attempted a translation of the complete Bible from the original languages include Moffatt, Beck, and Peterson. More commonly, individual translations of the complete Bible are a revision of an existing translation. For example, Knox used the Vulgate, both the *Amplified Bible* and the *Living Bible* are based on the *American Standard Version*, and both the *King James II* and the 21st *Century King James Version* are based on the *King James Version*.

The *King James Version* was the first English translation to be translated by a committee, which may have contributed to its superiority. The primary strength of a committee is that it brings a greater pool of talent to the task of translating. Since the 1970s, committees have produced the majority of the translations and, probably, will continue to do so in the future.

Most translations upon publication have had their share of critics and have been charged with theological bias. Jerome was criticized for being overly sympathetic to the Jews when he used the Hebrew Scriptures instead of the Septuagint to serve as a basis for his Old Testament. The *King James Version* has repeatedly been attacked for having a Calvinistic bias [Lewis, *English Bible*, 62]. The *Revised Standard Version* was strongly condemned by theological conservatives because of the liberal orientation of some of its translators. [In fact, it appears that the growth of translations produced by evangelicals can be partially attributed to the belief that the RSV has a liberal slant.] The *New American Standard Bible* was discredited simply because it was sponsored by the same organization that produced the *Amplified Bible*! All translations will, to varying extents, be biased for the simple reason that translating is a human activity.

Translation bias is most likely to occur with an individual translator who is overly swayed by his personal preferences. A committee of translators often provides balance for each other. However, committees can also display translation bias if all the committee members share the same religious perspective.

1) For example, the *New World Translation* (NWT) produced by Jehovah's Witnesses strongly denies the deity of Christ. Consider the following passages from the NWT:

   John 1:1   *In [the] beginning the Word was, and the Word was with God, and the Word was a god.*

   Philippians 2:6   *who, although he was existing in God's form, gave no consideration to a seizure, namely, that he should be equal to God.*

   Colossians 1:16-17   *...because by means of him all [other] things were created...All [other] things have been created through him and for him. Also, he is before all [other] things and by means of him all [other] things were made to exist.*

   Titus 2:13   *while we wait for the happy hope and glorious manifestation of the great God and of [the] Savior of us, Christ Jesus.*

2) As another example, the early editions of the NASB translated Matthew 16:19 as *"...whatever you bind on earth shall have been bound in heaven, and whatever you shall loose on earth shall have been loosed in heaven."* All other major translations read *"shall be bound"* and *"shall be loosed"*. Is this an example of Protestant bias, or a valid disagreement on the appropriate translation? Later editions of the NASB changed to read as other translations. However, the NASB (1995) and NASB (2020) reverts to its original reading!

The number of translators and theological orientation of some of the major committee translations are as follows:

Version	No. of Translators	Theological Orientation	Publisher
King James Version	54 (or 47)	Protestant (Anglican)	
Revised Standard Version	65	Protestant	Cambridge, Oxford, Nelson
New English Bible	26 or 46?	Protestant (Catholic Observers)	Cambridge, Oxford
Jerusalem and New Jerusalem Bible	27	Roman Catholic	Doubleday
New American Standard Bible	54	Evangelical	Cambridge, Holman, Moody, Nelson, et.al.
New American Bible	55	50 Catholic 5 Protestant	Macmillan, Nelson
New International Version	40 or 115?	Evangelical	NY Bible Society, Oxford, Zondervan
New King James Version	119	Evangelical	Nelson
New Revised Standard Version	30	Protestant, Catholic, 1 Greek Orthodox, 1 Jew	Cambridge, Oxford
Revised English Bible	26	Protestant and Catholic	Cambridge, Oxford
New Living Translation	90	Evangelical	Tyndale House

It has often been asserted that a faithful translation can only be produce by translators who believe in the verbal inspiration and inerrancy of the Scriptures. It is contended that only such translators will have the proper respect for the text and that if a translator does not hold the text in this high of a regard there will be a tendency on his part to manipulate the text. This may very well be true. However, consider this. A 'liberal' person will hold his views regardless of what the text says. They simply don't believe the text. Whereas, the 'conservative' person believes the text and has a great deal at stake in what the text says. From this perspective, who has an interest in the text that may tempt them to change the text? The conservative. Translations should be judged on their translation and not on their translators.

Target Reader

All translators have in mind an intended reader and attempt to produce a translation that is clearly understood by their intended reader.

Children   Many translations have been developed for children or teenagers: The *Children's Version of the Holy Bible* (1962), *Children's New Testament* (1969), *International Children's Bible* (1986; *New Century Version*), and *New International Reader's Version* (1995). These versions tend to limit the vocabulary and simplify the sentence structure.

The relative ease of understanding a translation is seen by the 'reading grade level' assigned to the translation. The reading grade level reflects the level of education required to understand the translation. The reading grade level of several current translations is as follows:

King James Version	12.00	Today's English Version	7.29
New American Standard Bible	11.32	New American Bible	6.60
New Revised Standard Version	10.40	New Living Translation	6.30
English Standard Version	10.00	God's Word	5.80
New King James Version	9.00	Contemporary English Version	5.40
The Living Bible	8.33	The Message	4.80
New International Version	7.80	International Children's Bible	3.90
Holman Christian Standard	7.50	New International Reader's Version	2.90

English as Second Language   Several translations have been designed for readers that have English as a second language. Around 1950, two English translations appeared in a simplified form of English: *The Basic Bible* (1949) and the *New Testament in Plain English* (1952). *Basic English* had a vocabulary limited to 850 words. For this translation, 150 other words were added. 'Plain English' was a simplified system with 1,500 words, and an additional 160+ others were used in the translation. The limited vocabulary may have made it more accessible to a new English reader, but it also resulted in some unnatural translations.

Public Reading   A Bible designed for public reading must be aware of how the translation is heard. For example, the *New Revised Standard Version* (a revision of the *Revised Standard Version*) was designed for both private and public use. So, being aware of possible confusions in oral reading the following changes were made (cf. Metzger, *Making of NRSV*, 68):

Genesis 35:7	RSV	*Because there God had revealed himself.*
	NRSV	*Because it was there that God had revealed himself.*
Luke 22:35	RSV	*"Did you lack anything?" They said, "Nothing."*
	NRSV	*"Did you lack anything?" They said, "No, not a thing."*

Catholic Catholic productions such as the *New Jerusalem Bible* and the *New American Bible* are clearly intended primarily for Catholics. Yet, even the essentially Protestant Bibles such as the *New Revised Standard Version* and the *Revised English Bible* produce editions that include the Apocrypha to appeal to Catholic readers.

Text Selection

Most recent translations have used the standard critical Hebrew (*Biblia Hebraica Stuttgartensia*) and Greek (*The Greek New Testament* or *Novum Testamentum Graece*) texts as a starting point for their translation. The translators will then make their own judgments on the variant manuscript readings. In the Old Testament, readings from the Septuagint or the Dead Sea Scrolls may be given precedence over the Masoretic text. In the New Testament, different translators will give different weight to each of the variant readings. Consequently, no two translations will be based on the exact same Hebrew and Greek texts. This fact alone suggests that multiple translations should be consulted for study purposes.

For translations of the Old Testament, knowledge from secular sources has at times influenced the translation. For example, the KJV rendering of 2 Kings 23:29 is "*In his days Pharoahnechoh king of Egypt went up against the king of Assyria to the river Euphrates...*" More recent discoveries (the Babylonian Chronicles) have informed us that Necho actually went up to assist Assyria. Thus, the Hebrew expression translated '*went up against*' should rather be translated "*went up to assist*". The NKJV reads "*In his days Pharoah Necho king of Egypt went to the aid of the king of Assyria, to the River Euphrates...*" Other translations (e.g., NASB and NRSV) simply say that Necho "*went up to*" the king of Assyria. In either case, it is clear that Necho did not go up "*against*" the king of Assyria.

In the New Testament, the modern critical texts are more likely to omit a word or phrase that was found in the KJV than to add text. For example, in 45 cases the NIV omits words, phrases or verses found in the KJV [Lewis, 304]. The two most noteworthy are the ending of Mark (Mark 16:9-20) and the story of the woman caught in adultery (John 8:1-11). Modern critical texts omit both of these accounts. Even so, most translations will still include them and also include a marginal note that they are in later manuscripts (NASB), or place them within brackets with a marginal note (NRSV), or will print the account at the end of the book (REB).

The Genuineness of Mark 16:9-20

Most modern translations give some sort of indication that the last twelve verses of Mark are not contained in the earliest Greek manuscripts. Nevertheless, they all have decided to include these verses. There are other verses or groups of verses in the New Testament whose genuineness are questioned (e.g., John 8:1-11, Acts 8:37), but the ending of Mark has generated the most attention. However, there is nothing taught in these twelve verses that is not taught or illustrated in other portions of the New Testament.

The textual evidence is more complicated than simply whether or not the last twelve verses were part of Mark's Gospel. There are four different endings to Mark's Gospel attested in various Greek manuscripts:

(continued on the next page)

---

1) The two oldest, major Greek manuscripts in our possession, Sinaiticus (א) and Vaticanus (B), come from the fourth century. Neither of these manuscripts contain the last twelve verses of Mark. In addition, one of the earliest versions (a version is a translation of the Greek text into another language), the Sinaitic Syraic manuscript, does not contain these verses, nor do about 100 Armenian manuscripts or the two oldest Georgian manuscripts (ninth century). Both Eusebius (AD 339) and Jerome (AD 420) comment that the majority of Greek manuscripts known to them did not contain these verses; nevertheless, Jerome did include them in the Vulgate.

2) Although the last twelve verses of Mark (called the "longer ending" of Mark) are not included in the two oldest manuscripts they are included in three important fifth century Greek manuscripts: the Codex Alexandrinus, Ephraemi Rescriptus, and the Codex Washingtonianus. The Alexandrinus manuscript is especially held in high regard and at times modern critical textual scholars have preferred its reading above that of the Sinaiticus and Vaticanus. About 99% of all known Greek manuscripts include these verses (although some have scribal notes stating that older Greek manuscripts lack these verses). More important, Irenaeus quotes from Mark 16:19 in the second century (over 100 years earlier than the Sinaiticus manuscript).

3) Several late Greek manuscripts of the seventh century and later have what is called the "shorter ending" of Mark following verse 8. It states *"But they reported briefly to Peter and those with him all that they had been told. And after this Jesus himself sent out by means of them, from east to west, the sacred and imperishable proclamation of eternal salvation."* Nearly all of these manuscripts then continue with verses 9-20. No scholar argues that the shorter ending is genuine.

4) The Codex Washingtonianus noted above as including verses 9-20 also has another section of text inserted after verse 14. This additional text clearly has no claims to being original.

On the basis of the textual evidence alone, most scholars would acknowledge that it is very possible that the text of verses 9-20 is genuine. However, the vast majority of scholars do not believe them to be genuine when internal evidences are also considered. They argue that the style and vocabulary of verses 9-20 is drastically different than the earlier sections of Mark which to them suggests a different author (but decisions based on style/vocabulary are always dubious). However, scholars are divided between the opinion that the original ending of Mark was lost (since they cannot conceive of the Gospel ending with verse 8) and the opinion that Mark indeed did intend to end his Gospel with verse 8 (which seems to be getting more recent support, even among evangelical scholars).

So, are verses 9-20 genuine? The only possible answer is that we do not know. Even if they are not genuine, all would agree that they were added at a very early date.

Lesson 11

Translation Issues (II)

Introduction

Most of us are indebted to translators for providing the Scriptures in a language that we can read and understand. Throughout history, as illustrated by the times of Josiah, Ezra, or the Reformation, the written word of God has forcefully impacted men's lives.

Translation Philosophy

All translators have a translating philosophy that guides them in their work. There are two broad approaches or philosophies of translation.

1) A translator may believe that the best translation is one that maintains the *form* or structure of the original document. This approach has been variously named *formal equivalence*, *verbal equivalence*, *word-for-word*, or *literal*.

2) Another translator may contend that the best translation is one that conveys the same *meaning* as the original document, which may require modifying the form. This approach is commonly called *dynamic equivalence, functional equivalence, meaning-for-meaning*, or *free*. Paraphrases are an extreme example of this approach.

Since there is significant latitude within each approach and translators may even vary their approach within their translation, it is difficult to uniformly classify existing translations. Interestingly, even the very first translation, the Septuagint, has portions that would be classified as literal translation (e.g., Judges, Psalms) and as free translation (e.g., Proverbs, Isaiah) [Metzger, *Translation*, 17]. The following relative classification is just "one man's opinion." Compare with Carson's "sliding scale" from "more formal translations" to "more functional translations": ASV, NASB, KJV, NKJV, RSV, NRSV, NJB, NIV, NIVI, NLT, CEV, LB [*Inclusive Language Debate*, 17].

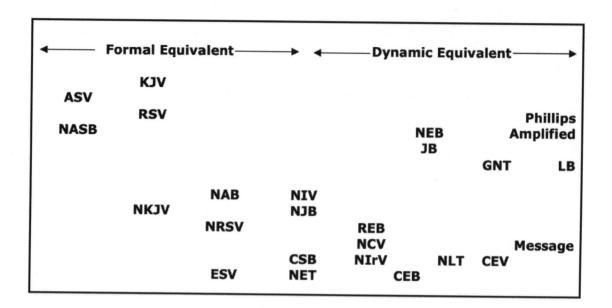

The variation in translations can be seen in their handling of **Philippians 2:6-7a**:

KJV

Who, being in the form of God, thought it not robbery to be equal with God: But made himself of no reputation, and took upon him the form of a servant, ...

ASV (RSV sim.)

who, existing in the form of God, counted not the being on an equality with God a thing to be grasped, but emptied himself, taking the form of a servant, ...

NASB

who, as He already existed in the form of God, did not consider equality with God something to be grasped, but emptied Himself by taking the form of a bond-servant, ...

NIV

Who, being in very nature God, did not consider equality with God something to be used to his own advantage; rather, he made himself nothing by taking the very nature of a servant, ...

NRSV

who, though he was in the form of God, did not regard equality with God as something to be exploited, but emptied himself, taking the form of a slave, ...

REB

He was in the form of God; yet he laid no claim to equality with God, but made himself nothing, assuming the form of a slave.

GNT

He always had the very nature of God, but he did not think that by force he should try to become equal with God. Instead, of his own free will he gave it all up, and took the nature of a servant.

PHILLIPS

For he, who had always been God by nature, did not cling to his prerogatives as God's equal, but stripped himself of all privilege by consenting to be a slave by nature...

JB

His state was divine, yet he did not cling to his equality with God, but emptied himself to assume the condition of a slave, ...

NCV

Christ himself was like God in everything. But he did not think that being equal with God was something to be used for his own benefit. But he gave up his place with God and made himself nothing. ... and became like a servant.

CSB

Who, existing in the form of God, did not consider being equality with God as something to be exploited. Instead he emptied Himself by assuming the form of a servant, ...

ESV

who, though he was in the form of God, did not count equality with God a thing to be grasped, but emptied himself, by taking the form of a servant, ...

Things to Consider

1. There is no such thing as a word-for-word translation. The closest thing is the English sub-text given in a Greek-English interlinear. Next to that, there are literal translations. In fact, two have been recently published: 1) *Literal English Version* (2016) based on the *World English Bible*, 2) *Literal Standard Version* (2020) based on *Young's Literal* translation. For example, compare Acts 5:32-35a with Berry's Interlinear, the *Literal Standard Version* (LSV), and the NKJV.

Berry's Interlinear

And we are of him witnesses of things these and the Spirit also the Holy which gave God to those that obey him. But they having heard were cut and took counsel to put to death them. Having risen up but a certain in the Sanhedrin a Pharisee by name Gamaliel a teacher of the law honored by all the people commanded out for a short while the apostles to put and said to them...

Literal Standard Version

... and we are His witnesses of these sayings, and the Holy Spirit also, whom God gave to those obeying Him. And they having heard, were cut [to the heart], and were intending to slay them, but a certain one, having risen up in the Sanhedrin – a Pharisee, by name Gamaliel, a teacher of the law honored by all the people – commanded to put the apostles forth a little, and said to them, ...

NKJV

"And we are His witnesses to these things, and so also is the Holy Spirit whom God has given to those who obey Him." When they heard *this*, they were furious and plotted to kill them. Then one in the council stood up, a Pharisee named Gamaliel, a teacher of the law held in respect by all the people, and commanded them to put the apostles outside for a little while. And he said to them...

NLT

"We are witnesses of these things and so is the Holy Spirit, who is given by God to those who obey him." When they heard this, the high council was furious and decided to kill them. But one member, a Pharisee named Gamaliel, who was an expert in religious law and respected by all the people, stood up and ordered that the men be sent outside the council chamber for a while. Then he said to his colleagues...

The most obvious difference is the word order. Different languages have different rules regarding word order. Word order is more important in English for understandability than it is in Greek. Also, it will be noticed that the English translation must add words to complete the sense. The NKJV follows the practice first started by the *Geneva Bible* of italicizing any additional words. The KJV, ASV, and NASB also follow this practice. However, this is a difficult policy to implement and reviewers of these translations have commented on their inconsistency in application.

Attempts to maintain the Greek word order can lead to ambiguities. For example, the ASV of Acts 14:6, following the literal word order of the Greek, reads "*and fled unto the cities of Lycaonia, Lystra and Derbe …*". The natural reading of this would suggest that three cities are being listed. But Lycaonia is not a city. So, it is best to modify the word order for clarity. Thus, the KJV reads "*fled unto Lystra and Derbe, cities of Lycaonia, …*" and the REB reads "*fled to the Lycaonian cities of Lystra and Derbe.*"

2. Idioms cannot be translated directly from one language to another without a possible loss of understanding. For example, among the Hebrews the "bowels" were considered the seat of emotions. Thus, in Colossians 3:12 Christians are exhorted to "*put on*" "*bowels of mercies*" (KJV). The NASB (a 'literal' translation) translates that expression "*heart of compassion*"; similarly, the ESV has "*compassionate hearts*". An English idiom has been used to express a Hebrew idiom. The NRSV avoids an idiomatic expression altogether and simply translates "*compassion*".

3. Cultural norms are also difficult to translate literally. Jesus' address to his mother as "*Woman*" (KJV, NKJV, NASB, NRSV, JB, ESV, NABRE, NET) in John 2:4 seems harsh to us. Yet, in the Jewish culture of Jesus' day, it was a common expression of affection. Thus, some versions translate "*dear woman*" (NIV, NCV), "*mother*" (NEB, CEV), or just avoid the issue by omitting the term altogether (REB, LB).

4. Some expressions are ambiguous in the original and can take on more than one meaning. There are several examples in 1 Corinthians. Consider the following: (see additional examples charted at the end of this lesson)

   a. 1 Corinthians 2:13b is literally translated "*comparing spiritual things with spiritual*" (KJV). The expression is incomplete: comparing with spiritual *what*? A common interpretation is "spiritual *words*" (ASV, NASB, NIV sim.). But not all translations agree: NRSV, ESV "*interpreting spiritual things to those who are spiritual*"; REB "*interpreting spiritual truths to those who have the Spirit.*"

   b. 1 Corinthians 8:3 literally translated is "*but if any man loveth God, the same is known by him*" (ASV). The uncertainty is to whom does "*the same*" and "*him*" refer? Essentially all versions identify "*the same*" with the "*man*" and identify "*him*" with "*God*". To my knowledge, only Goodspeed reverses the identification. The interesting point is that only the KJV and the ASV leave the ambiguity in their translation. All others in essence (including 'literal' translations) remove the ambiguity in favor of one option.

5. The main concern with the dynamic equivalence approach is that in the effort to convey the same meaning, does the translator truly know the meaning of the original author or is he promoting an interpretation foreign to the text? The checks and balances typical of a committee translation may help to limit improper interpreting.

6. Most modern translations acknowledge that a balance is required between formal equivalence and dynamic equivalence. Thus, the policy of the NRSV translators

was to be "as literal as possible, as free as necessary." ESV summarizes a similar approach with the phrase "essentially literal," and CSB uses the expression "optimal equivalence." This is probably the best that can be asked of a translator.

Suggestion

A good practice is to use at least three translations.

(1) Since many are still most familiar with the language of the *King James Version*, it would be wise to maintain contact with this tradition by using either the *King James Version* itself or the *New King James Version*.

(2) As a basis for detailed study, use a modern formal equivalent translation such as the ASV, RSV, NASB, NRSV, ESV, CSB, or NAB.

(3) For comparative purposes, use a dynamic equivalent translation such as the NET, NIV, REB, NLT, NJB, or CEB.

Translation Format

The format of the translation can serve multiple useful purposes. Without doubt, the greatest aid has been the subdividing of text into chapters and verses.

> "The traditional division of chapters (previously ascribed to Hugh of St. Cher and dated about 1262) is now attributed to Stephen Langton, a Lecturer at the University of Paris and subsequently Archbishop of Canterbury (d.1228). The present method employed for verses was originated by the scholarly printer Robert Stephanus (Estienne), whose Greek New Testament with numbered verses was issued in Geneva in 1551. The first English Bible to employ Stephanus's system of numbering verses was the Geneva version (New Testament 1556; Old Testament 1560)." [Metzger, "Bible", 79-80]

The *King James Version* followed the *Geneva Bible* in printing each verse as a separate paragraph, however, to help the reader, a ¶ symbol was placed at the beginning of each "true" paragraph. Curiously though, this practice was stopped after Acts 20. The *New American Standard Bible* continued this practice with the addition of bolding the verse number at the start of the paragraph. The *New King James Version* dropped the ¶ symbol, but bolds the verse number. Most translations will print the text as paragraphs and still retain the verse numbering within the text or in the margin. Some paraphrases omit verse numbering (e.g., Phillips). As one might expect, the various translations do not agree in paragraph divisions. Translators must use their judgment in this matter that is based on their understanding of the text.

Beginning with the ASV, modern translations distinguish the poetic sections of Scripture by printing them in lines, stanzas, etc.

The *New American Standard Bible* started the practice (to the best of my knowledge) of identifying the portions of the New Testament text that are quotations of the Old Testament with small capital letters. The *New King James Version* continues this practice, but uses an oblique font. The CSB carries this practice further by using a bold font even if the quote is not introduced as being from the Old Testament (e.g., Romans 2:6). Many modern translations will use quotation marks to delineate Old Testament quotations if they are introduced by "*It is written*", or some such indicator (e.g., NRSV, ESV). One translation (Beck's) italicizes portions of the Old Testament that are quoted in the New Testament.

The use of red letters to indicate the speech of Jesus originated with Dr. Louis Klopsch in his *Red Letter New Testament* (1899), and it was soon adopted in the printing of many *King James Versions*.

A similar practice of using quotation marks to indicate direct speech was introduced by the *Revised Standard Version* and is followed by most (if not all) recent translations. Again, the judgment of the translator is required in determining what is or is not direct speech.

Examples

1. Jesus begins speaking in John 3:10, but does his speech conclude in verse 15 (RSV) or verse 21 (most translations, including NRSV)?

2. In Galatians 2, does Paul's speech to Peter conclude in verse 15 or verse 21? Compare various translations.

Ambiguities in 1 Corinthians

Passage	Literal / KJV	Question	ASV	NKJV
2:13	"comparing spiritual things with spiritual" KJV	What is the appropriate noun for the modifier "spiritual"?	"... with spiritual *words*"	"comparing spiritual things with spiritual"
3:9	"For of God we are co-workers" Lit.	Can mean either working *with* God or *for* God.	"God's fellow-workers"	"God's fellow workers"
5:4	"I have already judge the one having done this thing in the name of the Lord Jesus you being gathered ..." Lit.	Refers to Paul's authority, the Corinthian assembly, or the delivering of man?	"this thing, in the name..., ye being gathered... to deliver such a one..."	"In the name..., when you are gathered ... , deliver such a one ..."
5:5	"to deliver" KJV	Paul or the Corinthians or both could be the subject of "deliver".	"to deliver..."	"deliver"
7:1	"It is good for a man not to touch a woman." KJV	What does "not to touch a woman mean?	"It is good for a man not to touch a woman."	"it is good for a man not to touch a woman."
7:21	"if indeed you can become free, use it rather" Lit.	Mean either to use one's slave condition or to use opportunity to be free.	"even if you canst become free, use it rather" (also KJV)	"but if you can become free, rather use it"
12:1	"Now concerning spiritual things" Lit.	Does "things" refer to "gifts" or "people"?	"Now concerning spiritual *gifts*" (also KJV)	"Now concerning spiritual *gifts*"

Passage	NRSV	REB	NASB	ESV
2:13	"interpreting spiritual things to those who are spiritual"	"interpreting spiritual truths to those who have the Spirit"	"comparing spiritual *thoughts* with spiritual *words*"	"interpreting spiritual truths to those who are spiritual"
3:9	"we are God's servants, working together"	"We are fellow workers in God's service"	"God's fellow workers"	"God's fellow workers"
5:4	" ... I have already pronounced judgment in the name... on the man..."	"... I were indeed present: when you are assembled in the name..."	"... I were present. In the name..., when you are assembled ..."	"... such a thing. When you are assembled in the name..."
5:5	"you are to hand this man over to Satan..."	"you are to consign this man to Satan..."	"*I have decided* to turn such a person over ..."	"you are to deliver..."
7:1	"It is well for a man not to touch a woman"	"It is a good thing for a man to not have intercourse with a woman."	"It is good for a man not to touch a woman."	"It is good for a man not to have sexual relations with a woman."
7:21	"Even if you can gain your freedom, make use of your present condition..."	"though if a chance of freedom should come, by all means take it"	"but if you are able also to become free, take advantage of *that*"	"(But if you can gain your freedom, avail yourself of the opportunity.)"
12:1	"Now concerning spiritual gifts"	"About gifts of the Spirit"	"Now concerning spiritual *gifts*"	"Now concerning spiritual gifts"

Lesson 12

Translation Issues (III)

Introduction

Translators have a difficult task and their work often goes unappreciated. The same could be said for the archaeologist and the textual critic. But all are needed in providing us with a reliable, readable Bible.

Names and Pronouns for God

In an earlier lesson (Lesson 3), it was noted that the Jews refrained from speaking the name of God, which modern scholars believe should be written Yahweh. Instead, when reading the Scriptures, they would substitute "Lord" for his name. Most translations of the Old Testament have adopted a similar approach and write the word LORD (or, sometimes, GOD; both in small capitals) in place of God's name. The *American Standard Version* is unique among modern translations in rendering his name as Jehovah (except, of course, for the Jehovah's Witness' *New World Translation*), which is a composite name made up of the consonants of 'Yahweh' and the vowels of 'Lord' (*adonai*). The term Jehovah was first used by the Reformers, but is generally not used today. To the best of my knowledge, only the *New Jerusalem Bible* and the *World English Bible* use Yahweh.

English, during the time of the *King James*, contained the common pronouns *thee*, *thou*, *ye*, *thy*, and *thine* which were used in reference to both human and divine persons. These are no longer a part of modern English (which is somewhat unfortunate since the difference between the second person singular (*thou*) and second person plural (*ye*) is often useful in facilitating understanding). Out of respect for God, both the ASV and the RSV retained these pronouns (as did the NASB until the 1995 update edition) in speech directed toward God. This practice may be respectful, but it makes a distinction not made in the original writings. Thus, all recent translations have abandoned these pronouns and simply uses *you* or *your*. However, a few translations (NASB, NKJV) have adopted the practice of capitalizing all pronouns (e.g., He, Him, His, You, Your, etc.) referring to deity.

1. What could be problematic with capitalizing pronouns referring to deity?

Gender

Of all the translation issues currently debated, the issues involving gender generate the most discussion. This discussion may have been originally related to the feminist movement, but now related to the broader issues of gender in current discussion. It is a fact that the masculine gender is being used less as a generic reference to both men and women both in our writing and in our speech. Thus, most recent translations (NJB, NCV, NRSV, REB, NABRE, GNB, The Message, CEV, GW, NLT, NIVI, NIrV, CEB, CSB) seek to be "gender-inclusive." On the simplest level, the "gender-inclusive" versions seek "to capture the inclusive sense intended by the original author" (Strauss, *Distorting Scripture*, 60). Consider the following:

1. In Greek (like traditional English), the masculine gender is used as a generic reference to include both men and women. For example, Galatians 3:11 states "Now it is evident that no man is justified before God by the law" (RSV). Clearly, both men and women are intended, so the NRSV translates "Now it is evident that no one is justified before God by the law."

2. Our English translations will occasionally introduce the masculine gender when it is not in the original. For example, in Matthew 18:2, the KJV says *"And Jesus called a little child unto him, and set him in the midst of them, …"* The Greek text does not indicate the gender of the child [Metzger, *Making of NRSV*, 55], but many of our translations suggest that it was a boy (KJV, ASV, RSV, NASB, NKJV, NABRE, REB). Other recent translations render the latter part of the verse as *"and he set the child in front of them"* (JB; NRSV, NCV sim.). The question is whether a reader would understand the masculine pronoun to be a generic or to actually denote the sex of the child.

3. One tactic used by gender-inclusive versions is to replace the singular masculine term with a plural generic.

    a. For example, Matthew 16:24 reads *"Then Jesus told his disciples, "If anyone would come after me, let him deny himself and take up his cross and follow me."* (ESV). The NRSV renders the last phrase *"…let them deny themselves and take up their cross…"*.

    b. To use the plural in lieu of a singular does not necessarily mean that the translation is being unfaithful to the original text. The same phenomenon can be seen in NT quotations of OT passages.

        Isaiah 52:7 *"How beautiful upon the mountains are the feet of <u>him</u> who brings good news…"* (ESV)

        Romans 10:15b *"As it is written, 'How beautiful are the feet of <u>those</u> who preach the good news!'"* (ESV)

4. At other times it is difficult to know whether the term "*men*" is inclusive or not. This is particularly the case in historical narratives. For example, in Acts 4:4, had the church grown to 5,000 "*men*" (CSB, NLT, GW, NV) or (implied) 5,000 'persons' (CEB, NCV, NRSV, GNT, CEV)? The gender-inclusive versions are divided.

Consider also Romans 8:14: "*For all who are led by the Spirit of God are sons of God*" (ESV). Does Paul intend "*sons*" in the sense of "*children*" (thus, NRSV, etc.)? Perhaps. This would make the passage consistent with v.21 where Paul explicitly says "*children of God*". But, could it be that Paul is intentionally trying to draw a parallel with the "*Son of God*" who was "*led by the Spirit*" in the wilderness (cf. Lk 4)? [see Edith Humphrey, 255]

5. Paul often uses the term "*brothers*" in his letters. The Greek term can, in some contexts, include women. So, gender-inclusive versions seek to replace "*brothers*" with a more gender-inclusive term.

   a. Consider the NRSV choices in the following passages:

Romans 8:3	"*my brothers*"	→	"*my kindred*"
1 Corinthians 1:10	"*my brothers*"	→	"*my brothers and sisters*"
Galatians 4:12	"*brothers*"	→	"*friends*"
Ephesians 6:23	"*to the brothers*"	→	"*to the whole community*"

   b. However, the context may not demand the generic. Note the following translations of James 3:1:

   "*Let not many of you become teachers, my brethren, for you know that we who teach shall be judged with greater strictness.*" RSV, ESV sim.

   "*Not many of you should become teachers, my brothers and sisters, for you know...*" NRSV

   "*Dear brothers and sisters, not many of you should become teachers in the church...*" NLT

   Given the teaching of other New Testament passages concerning the role of women, the NLT translation seems clearly inaccurate: "*in the church*" is not in the original text.

More extreme are versions such as the *New Testament and Psalms: An Inclusive Version* (NTPI) and the *Inclusive New Testament* (INT). These translations openly acknowledge that they change the text of Scripture to make it more in line with their theology. They seek to remove all gender terminology, except where it refers to a historical person. They do this in several ways:

   1. Masculine pronouns referring to God (and Satan) are eliminated. God is identified as "*Father-Mother*" or with generic expressions such as "*Abba God*"

in lieu of "*Father*". Jesus is not called "*Son*", but "*Only Begotten*", "*Firstborn*", etc.

2. The genealogies in Matthew 1 are modified to include the wives of the men if known. Thus, "*Abraham and Sarah were the parents of Isaac*" (Mt 1:2, NTPI).

3. They modify passages that in anyway suggest that a woman is subordinate to a man. Thus, in Ephesians 5:22, wives are not instructed to be "*subject*" to their husbands, but to "*be committed to*" husbands (NTPI).

4. Both the CEV and CEB remove all masculine references to the qualifications for elders and deacons in 1 Timothy 3 and Titus 1.

Obviously, such translations are not seeking to render what the original texts say, but what they think the original text means or should mean. As Dentan, a translator of the NRSV, remarked in explaining why the NRSV did not remove the patriarchal language used in reference to God: "*The Bible is a historical document, and the function of a scholar is to transmit the ancient text as faithfully as possible, not to adapt it to contemporary tastes*" [*Making of NRSV*, 6]. Ignoring the text may be the ultimate end of the dynamic equivalent approach in Biblical translating.

Weights and Measures

A continuing problem in translation is deciding how to translate weights and measures for things such as distances, weights, volumes, money, etc. In the first place, the exact equivalents of Biblical weights and measures are not known in our units of weights and measures so any conversion to our units can only be approximate. In many cases, the Biblical weight or measure varied from time to time or place to place (just like the value of a dollar varies today).

A second problem is that weights or measurements may be symbolic, and to convert these to our units would lose the symbolism. For example, in Revelation 21:15-17 the heavenly Jerusalem is measured. Each side was measured according to the NKJV as "*twelve thousand furlongs*" and its wall was "one hundred and forty-four cubits". The CEB reads "*fifteen hundred miles*" and "two *hundred sixteen feet,*" respectively. The NRSV translates the length of the side as "*fifteen hundred miles*", but then reverts and translates the wall as 144 cubits! Thankfully, the ESV retains the number symbolism with "*12,000 stadia*" and "*144 cubits*"!

A Concluding Word

The Bible has traveled an incredible journey from its initial composition to the multiple English translations now in our possession. The first writings were given to Israel. All the evidence suggests that the Jewish community carefully handled and transmitted these writings through the centuries, and there was little doubt which writings were considered Scripture.

The New Testament writings of the apostles and their associates were first passed among the churches, then copied and collected. From the beginning, they were esteemed as Scripture and placed alongside the Old Testament writings. In due course, they were translated into various languages, a challenging endeavor that underscored the immense value Christians placed on accessing these sacred writings.

As the number of handwritten manuscripts increased with each having some minor differences in readings, judgments had to be made to distinguish the original readings from the variant readings. The result? Scholars are in near universal agreement that the Greek text used as the basis of our English New Testament is a reliable reproduction of the original autographs. While a few readings lack certainty, these do not significantly hinder our understanding of God and his will.

It is impossible not to be thankful to those who faithfully preserved and transmitted the Biblical writings. Yet, our deepest thanks are reserved for our God who chose to reveal himself and his will first through his prophets, then fully through his Son and his chosen apostles.

"Thank you, Lord, for the gift of the Bible."

Biblical Quotations

English Standard Version. Unless otherwise indicated, all Scripture quotations are from the ESV® Bible (The Holy Bible, English Standard Version®), copyright © 2001 by Crossway, a publishing ministry of Good News Publishers. Used by permission. All rights reserved.

Other biblical quotations are taken from the following translations:

American Standard Bible. Scripture quotations marked (ASV) are taken from the American Standard Bible, 1901. Public Domain.

The Christian Standard Bible. Scripture quotations marked (CSB) are taken from the Christian Standard Bible, Copyright © 2017 by Holman Bible Publishers. Used by permission. Christian Standard Bible®, and CSB® are federally registered trademarks of Holman Bible Publishers, all rights reserved.

Common English Bible. Scripture quotations marked (CEB) from the Common English Bible. © Copyright 2011 Common English Bible. All rights reserved. Used by permission. (www.CommonEnglishBible.com).

Contemporary English Version. Scripture quotations marked (CEV) are from the Contemporary English Version Copyright © 1991, 1992, 1995 by American Bible Society. Used by Permission.

God's Word. All Scripture marked with the designation (GW) is taken from *GOD'S WORD*®. © 1995, 2003, 2013, 2014, 2019, 2020 by God's Word to the Nations Mission Society. Used by permission.

Good News Translation. Scripture quotations marked (GNT) are taken from Good News Translation® (Today's English Version, Second Edition). Copyright © 1992 American Bible Society. All rights reserved.

J. B. Phillips New Testament. Scripture quotations marked (Phillips) are taken from The New Testament in Modern English by J.B Phillips copyright © 1960, 1972 J. B. Phillips. Administered by The Archbishops' Council of the Church of England. Used by Permission.

Jerusalem Bible. Scripture quotations marked (JB) are taken from the JERUSALEM BIBLE Copyright© 1966, 1967, 1968 by Darton, Longmand & Todd LTD and Doubleday and Co. Inc. All rights reserved.

King James Version. Scripture quotations marked (KJV) are taken from the King James Version, 1611, 1769. Public Domain.

Literal Standard Version. Scripture quotations marked (LSV) are taken from The Literal Standard Version of The Holy Bible, a registered copyright of Covenant Press and the Covenant Christian Coalition (© 2020), subsequently released under the Creative Commons Attribution-ShareAlike license (CC BY-SA).

Revised English Bible. Scripture quotations marked (REB) taken from the Revised English Bible, copyright © Cambridge University Press and Oxford University Press 1989. All rights reserved.

Revised Standard Version. Scripture quotations marked (RSV) are taken from the Revised Standard Version of the Bible, copyright © 1946, 1952, and 1971 the Division of Christian Education of the National Council of the Churches of Christ in the United States of America. Used by permission. All rights reserved.

Tyndale New Testament. Scripture quotations marked (ASV) are taken from the Tyndale's translation of the New Testament, 1526. Public Domain.

World English Bible. Scripture quotations marked (WEB) are taken from the World English Bible, 2000. Public Domain.

Wycliffe Bible (1384). Scripture quotations marked (ASV) are taken from Wycliffe's translation of the Bible, 1384. Public Domain.

Bibliography

General

Ackroyd, P.R. and C.F. Evans, ed. *The Cambridge History of the Bible, Vol. I: From the Beginnings to Jerome*. Cambridge, 1970; G.W.H. Lampe, ed. *Vol. II: The West from the Fathers to the Reformation*. Cambridge, 1969; S.L. Greenslade, ed. *Vol III: The West from the Reformation to the Present Day*. Cambridge, 1963.

Armstrong, Karen. *The Bible: A Biography.* Atlantic Monthly Press, 2007.

Bratton, Fred Gladstone. *A History of the Bible: An Introduction to the Historical Method*. Beacon Press, 1959.

Bruce, F.F. *The Books and the Parchments: How We Got Our English Bible*. Fleming H. Revell Company, 1984.

_____. *The New Testament Documents: Are They Reliable?* Fifth Ed. IVP, 1960.

Colwell, Ernest Cadman. *The Study of the Bible*, Revised Ed. University of Chicago Press, 1964.

Comfort, Philip Wesley, ed. *The Origin of the Bible*. Tyndale House Publishers, 1992.

de Hamel, Christopher. *The Book: A History of the Bible*. Phaidon Press Limited, 2001.

Fee, Gordon D. and Douglas Stuart. *How to Read the Bible for All Its Worth: A Guide to Understanding the Bible*. Zondervan, 1982.

Fitzmyer, Joseph A. *Spiritual Exercises: Based on Paul's Epistle to the Romans.* Eerdmans, 1995.

Geisler, Norman L. and William E. Nix. *From God to Us: How We Got Our Bible*. Moody Press, 1974.

Gleaves, G. Scott. *Did Jesus Speak Greek? The Emerging Evidence of Greek Dominance in First Century Palestine.* Wipf and Stock Publishers, 2015.

Grudem, Wayne, C. John Collins, and Thomas R. Schreiner, eds. *Understanding Scripture: An Overview of the Bible's Origin, Reliability, and Meaning*. Crossway, 2012.

Harrell, Ed, ed. "The Bible," *Christianity Magazine*, Vol. 2, No. 9 (Sept. 1985)

Kenyon, Frederic. *Our Bible and the Ancient Manuscripts*, Fifth Ed. Harper and Row, 1958.

Kohlenberger, John R. *All About Bibles*. Oxford University Press, 1985.
Lightfoot, Neil R. *How We Got the Bible*, 3rd Ed. MJF Books, 2003 (1963, 1988)

McDonald, Lee Martin and Stanley E. Porter. *Early Christianity and Its Sacred Literature*. Hendrickson, 2000.

Metzger, Bruce M. and Michael D. Coogan, eds. *The Oxford Companion to the Bible*. Oxford University Press, 1993.

    Holmgren, Laton E. "Bible Societies," p. 80-82.

    Metzger, Bruce M. "Bible," p.78-80.

    _____. "Manuscripts," p. 486-490.

    Sanders, James A. "Masorah," p.500-501.

Patzia, Arthur G. *The Making of the New Testament: Origin, Collection, Text & Canon*. InterVarsity Press, 1995.

Peters, F.E. *The Voice, The Word, The Books: The Sacred Scripture of the Jews, Christians, and Muslims*. Princeton University Press, 2007.

Pelikan, Jaroslav. *Whose Bible Is It? A History of the Scriptures through the Ages*. Viking, 2005.

Pope, Kyle. *How We Got the Bible*. Ancient Road Publications, 2007.

Porter, Stanley E. *How We Got the New Testament: Text, Transmission, Translation*. Baker, 2013.

Price, Ira Maurice. *The Ancestry of Our English Bible: An Account of Manuscripts, Texts, and Versions of the Bible*, Third Revised Ed. by William A. Irwin and Allen P. Wikgren. Harper & Brothers, Publishers, 1956.

Quinn, Jon E. and Warren Berkley, eds. *The Integrity of the New Testament*. Expository Files, 2014.

Rogerson, John. *The Oxford Illustrated History of the Bible*. Oxford University Press, 2001.

Smyth, J. Patterson. *How We Got Our Bible*. Harper & Brothers Publishers, 1912.

Van der Toon, Karel. *Scribal Culture and the Making of the Hebrew Bible*. Harvard University Press, 2007.

Wegner, Paul D. *The Journey from Texts to Translations: The Origin and Development of the Bible*. Baker Books, 1999 (2nd printing, 2002).

Williams, James B. and Randolph Shaylor, eds. *God's Word in Our Hands: The Bible Preserved for Us*. Ambassador Emerald International, 2003.

Witherington, Ben III. *What's in the Word: Rethinking the Socio-Rhetorical Character of the New Testament*. Baylor University Press, 2009.

Ancient Writing

Alexander, Loveday. "Ancient Book Production and the Circulation of the Gospels," in *The Gospels for All Christians: Rethinking the Gospel Audiences*, ed. By Richard Bauckham. Eerdmans, 1998.

Gaur, Albertine. *A History of Writing*, Revised Edition. Cross River Press, 1992.

Holmes, Michael W. "Textual Criticism," in *New Testament Criticism an Interpretation*, ed. By David Alan Black and David S. Dockery. Zondervan, 1991.

Hyatt, J. Philip. "The Writing of an Old Testament Book," *The Biblical Archaeologist Reader*, Vol. I, ed. G. Ernst Wright and David Noel Freedman. Scholars Press, 1975.

Meyers, Eric M. ed. *The Oxford Encyclopedia of Archaeology in the Near East*. Oxford University Press, 1997.

> Anderson-Stojanovic, Virginia R. "Leather," Vol. 3, p.339-340.

> Bar-Ilan, Meir. "Papyrus," Vol. 4, p.246-247.

> Bar-Ilan, Meir. "Parchment," Vol. 4, p.247-248.

> Daniels, Peter T. "Writing and Writing Systems," Vol. 5, p.352-358.

> Daniels, Peter T. "Writing Materials," Vol. 5, p.358-361.

Millard, Alan. "Writing Tablets: Notepaper of the Roman World," *Biblical Archaeology Review*, Vol.29, No.4 (July/August 2003)

_____. "Zechariah Wrote (Luke 1:63)," *The New Testament in Its First Century Setting: Essays on Context and Background in Honour of B.W. Winter on His 65th Birthday*, P.J. Williams, Andrew D. Clarke, Peter M. Head, David Instone-Brewer, eds. Eerdmans, 2004.

Canon

Abraham, William J. *Canon and Criterion in Christian Theology*. Oxford University Press, 1998.

Allert, Craig D. *A High View of Scripture? The Authority of the Bible and the Formation of the New Testament Canon*. Baker Academic, 2007.

Bruce, F.F. *The Canon of Scripture*. InterVarsity Press, 1988.

deSilva, David A. *Introducing the Apocrypha: Message, Context, and Significance*. Baker Academic, 2002.

Dungan, David L. *Constantine's Bible: Politics and the Making of the New Testament*. SCM Press, 2006.

Ehrman, Bart D. *The Orthodox Corruption of Scripture: The Effect of Early Christological Controversies on the Text of the New Testament*. Oxford University Press, 1993.

_____. *Lost Christianities: The Battles for Scripture and Faiths We Never Knew*. Oxford University Press, 2003.

Evans, Craig A. and Emanuel Tov, eds. *Exploring the Origins of the Bible: Canon Formation in Historical, Literary, and Theological Perspective*. Baker Academic, 2008.

Harris, R. Laird. *Inspiration and Canonicity of the Bible: An Historical and Exegetical Study*. Zondervan, 1969.

Kaiser, Otto. *The Old Testament Apocrypha: An Introduction*. Hendrickson, 2004.

Kruger, Michael J. *Canon Revisited: Establishing the Origins and Authority of the New Testament Books*. Crossway, 2012.

_____. *The Question of Canon: Challenging the Status Quo in the New Testament Debate*. IVP Academic, 2013.

Kostenberger, Andreas J. and Michael J. Kruger. *The Heresy of Orthodoxy: How Contemporary Culture's Fascination with Diversity Has Reshaped our Understanding of Early Christianity*. Crossway, 2010.

Paher, Stanley W. *The Development of the New Testament Canon*. Nevada Publications, 1997.

McDonald, Lee Martin. *Forgotten Scriptures: The Selection and Rejection of Early Religious Writings*. Westminster John Knox, 2009.

_____. *Formation of the Bible: The Story of the Church's Canon*. Hendrickson, 2012.

McDonald, Lee Martin and James A. Sanders, eds. *The Canon Debate*. Hendrickson, 2002.

Metzger, Bruce M. *The Canon of the New Testament: Its Origin, Development, and Significance*. Oxford University Press, 1987.

_____. *An Introduction to the Apocrypha*. Oxford University Press, 1957.

Perrin, Nicholas. *Thomas, the Other Gospel*. Westminster John Knox Press, 2007.

Ridderbos, Herman N. *Redemptive History and the New Testament Scriptures*. Presbyterian and Reformed Publishing Company, 1963.

Sanders, James A. *From Sacred Story to Sacred Text*. Fortress Press, 1987.

Seitz, Christopher R. *This Goodly Fellowship of the Prophets: The Achievement of Association in Canon Formation.* Baker Academic, 2009.

Trobisch, David. *Paul's Letter Collection: Tracing the Origins*. Fortress, 1994.

Westcott, B.F. *A General Survey of the History of the Canon of the New Testament*, Sixth Ed. MacMillan and Company, 1889.

Textual Criticism

Aland, Kurt and Barbara Aland. *The Text of the New Testament*. Eerdmans, 1987.

Black, David Alan, ed. *Rethinking New Testament Textual Criticism*. Baker Academic, 2002.

_____. *Perspectives on the Ending of Mark: 4 Views*. B&H Academic, 2008.

Boltzman, Ellis R. *Old Testament Textual Criticism: A Practical Introduction*. Baker, 1994.

Colwell, Earnest C. *Studies in Methodology in Textual Criticism of the New Testament.* E.J.Brill, 1969.

Comfort, Philip. *Encountering the Manuscripts: An Introduction to New Testament Paleography and Textual Criticism.* B&H Publishers, 2005.

Epp, Eldon J. and Gordon D. Fee. *Studies in the Theory and Method of New Testament Textual Criticism*, *Studies and Documents*, Irving Alan Sparks, ed. Eerdmans, 1993.

Ehrman, Bart D. *The Orthodox Corruption of Scripture: The Effect of Early Christological Controversies on the Text of the New Testament.* Oxford University Press, 1993.

_____. *Misquoting Jesus: The Story Behind Who Changed the Bible and Why.* HarperSanFrancisco, 2005.

Finegan, Jack. *Encountering New Testament Manuscripts: A Working Introduction to Textual Criticism*. Eerdmans, 1974.

Friedman, Matti. *The Aleppo Codex: A True Story of Obsession, Faith, and the Pursuit of an Ancient Bible.* Algonquin Books of Chapel Hill, 2012.

Greenlee, J. Harold. *Scribes, Scrolls, and Scripture: A Student's Guide to New Testament Textual Criticism*. Eerdmans, 1985.

_____. *The Text of the New Testament: From Manuscripts to Modern Edition*. Hendrickson Publishers, 2008. [Revision and Expansion of Scribes, *Scrolls, and Scripture.*]

_____. *Introduction to New Testament Textual Criticism*, Revised Ed. Hendrickson, 1995.

Hamann, H.P. *A Popular Guide to New Testament Criticism*. Concordia Publishing House, 1977.

Hannah, Darrell. "New Testament Manuscripts: Uncials, Minuscules, Palimpsests, etc.," *Approaches to the Bible: The Best of Bible Review*, ed. By Harvey Minkoff. Biblical Archaeology Society, 1994.

Harrison, R.K., Waltke, B.K., Guthrie, D. and Fee, G.D. *Biblical Criticism*. Zondervan, 1978.

Hester, David W. *Does Mark 16:9-20 Belong in the New Testament?* Wipf & Stock, 2015.

Ladd, George Eldon. *The New Testament and Criticism*. Eerdmans, 1967.

Metzger, Bruce M. *The Text of the New Testament: Its Transmission, Corruption, and Restoration*, Second Ed. Oxford University Press, 1968.

Mounce, William D. "Do Formal Equivalent Translations Reflect a Higher View of Plenary, Verbal Inspiration?" *Themelios*, Vol.44, Issue 3, December 2019.

Ortlund, Dane. On Words, Meanings, Inspiration, and Translation." *Themelios*, Vol.45, Issue 1, April 2020.

Parker, David C. *Textual Scholarship and the Making of the New Testament.* Oxford University Press, 2012.

Porter, Stanley E. and Andrew W. Pitts. *Fundamentals of New Testament Textual Criticism*. Eerdmans, 2015. Kindle Edition.

Ramsay, William M. *St. Paul the Traveller and Roman Citizen*, 5th Ed. Hodder and Stoughton, 1897; Reprinted Broadman Press, 1979.

Roberts, Phil. "Should We Return to the Text of the King James Version," *A Tribute to Melvin D. Curry, Jr.*, Ferrell Jenkins, ed. Florida College Bookstore, 1997.

Soulen, Richard N. *Handbook of Biblical Criticism*, Second Ed. John Knox Press, 1976.

Stewart, Robert B., ed. *The Reliability of the New Testament: Bart D. Ehrman & Daniel B. Wallace in Dialogue*. Fortress Press, 2011.

Sturz, Harry A. *The Byzantine Text-Type and New Testament Criticism*. Thomas Nelson, 1984.

Thiede, Carsten Peter and Matthew D'Ancona. *The Jesus Papyrus*. Doubleday, 1996.

Wallace, Daniel B., ed. *Revisiting the Corruption of the New Testament: Manuscript, Patristic, and Apocryphal Evidence.* Kregal Publications, 2011.

Wegner, Paul D. *A Student's Guide to Textual Criticism of the Bible: Its History, Methods and Results*. InterVarsity Press, 2006.

Wurthwein, Ernst. *The Text of the Old Testament*. Eerdmans, 1979.

Dead Sea Scrolls

Bruce, F.F. "Recent Discoveries in Biblical Manuscripts," *Journal of the Transactions of the Victoria Institute* 82 (1950), p.131-149.

_____. *Second Thoughts on the Dead Sea Scrolls*, 2nd Ed. Eerdmans, 1961.

Charlesworth, James H. *The Pesharim and Qumran History: Chaos or Consensus?* Eerdmans, 2002.

Collins, John J. and Robert A. Kugler, eds. *Religion in the Dead Sea Scrolls*. Eerdmans, 2000.

Collins, John J. and Craig A. Evans, eds. *Christian Beginnings and he Dead Sea Scrolls.* Baker Academic, 2006.

Collins, John J. *The Dead Sea Scrolls: A Biography.* Princeton University Press, 2013.

Fitzmyer, Joseph A. *The Dead Sea Scrolls and Christian Origins*. Eerdmans, 2000.

_____. *The Impact of the Dead Sea Scrolls.* Paulist Press, 2009.

Flint, Peter, ed. *The Bible at Qumran: Text, Shape and Interpretation*. Eerdmans, 2001.

Hirschfeld, Yizhar. *Qumran in Context: Reassessing the Archaeological Evidence*. Hendrickson Publishers, 2004.

Lim, Timothy H. *The Dead Sea Scrolls: A Very Short Introduction*. Oxford University Press, 2005.

Magness, Jodi. *The Archaeology of Qumran and the Dead Sea Scrolls*. Eerdmans, 2002.

Shanks, Hershel, ed. *Understanding the Dead Sea Scrolls*. Random House, 1992.

Schiffman, Lawerance H. *Reclaiming the Dead Sea Scrolls*. EH Jewish Publication Society, 1994.

Shanks, Hershel, James C. Vanderkam, P. Kyle McCarter, Jr., and James A. Sanders. *The Dead Sea Scrolls After Forty Years*. Biblical Archaeology Society, 1992.

Vanderkim, James C. *The Dead Sea Scrolls Today*. Eerdmans, 1994.

VanderKam, James and Peter Flint. *The Meaning of the Dead Sea Scrolls*. HarperSanFrancisco, 2002.

Translations

Bailey, Lloyd R., ed. *The Word of God: A Guide to English Translations*. John Knox Press, 1982.

Barker, Kenneth L. *The Balance of the NIV: What Makes A Good Translation*. Baker, 1999.

Brake, Donald L. *A Visual History of the English Bible*. Baker, 2008.

Bruce, F.F. *History of the Bible in English*, Third Ed. Oxford University Press, 1978.

Brunn, Dave. *One Bible, Many Versions: Are All Translations Created Equal?* InterVarsity Press, 2012.

Campbell, Gordon. *Bible: The Story of the King James Version*. Oxford University Press, 2010.

Carson, D.A. *The King James Version Debate: A Plea for Realism*. Baker Book House, 1979.

_____. *The Inclusive Language Debate: A Plea for Realism*. Baker Books and Inter-Varsity Press, 1998.

Clendenen, E. Ray and David K. Stabnow. *The HCSB: Navigating the Horizons in Bible Translation*. B&H Publishing Group, 2012.

Comfort, Philip Wesley. *Early Manuscripts and Modern Translations of the New Testament.* Baker, 1990.

Daiches, David. *The King James Version of the English Bible.* Archon Books, 1968.

Daniell, David. *The Bible in English.* Yale University Press, 2003.

Dennett, Herbert. *A Guide to Modern Versions of the New Testament.* Moody Press, 1965.

Duthie, Alan S. *Bible Translations and How to Choose Between Them.* Paternoster Press, 1985.

Farstad, Arthur L. *The New King James Version in the Great Tradition.* Thomas Nelson, 1989.

Glassman, Eugene H. *The Translation Debate: What Makes a Bible Translation Good?* Intervarsity Press, 1982.

Goodspeed, Edgar J. *Problems of New Testament Translation.* University of Chicago Press, 1945.

Ferrell Jenkins. "The American Standard Version: Before and After," *A Tribute to Melvin D. Curry, Jr.*, Ferrell Jenkins, ed. Florida College Bookstore, 1997.

Humphrey, Edith M. "On Probabilities, Possibilities, and Pretexts: Fostering a Hermeneutics of Sobriety, Sympathy, and Imagination in an Impressionistic and Suspicious Age" in *Translating the New Testament: Text, Translation, Theology* by Stanley E. Porter and Mark J. Boda. Eerdmans, 2009.

Jeffrey, David Lyle, ed. *A Dictionary of Biblical Tradition in English Literature.* Eerdmans, 1992.

Jobes, Karen H. and Silva, Moises. *Invitation to the Septuagint.* Baker Academic, 2000.

Kostenberger, Andreas and David A. Croteau, eds. *Which Bible Translation Should I Use? A Comparison of Four Major Recent Versions.* B&H Publishing Group, 2012.

Kubo, Sakae and Walter F. Specht. *So Many Versions? 20th Century English Versions of the Bible.* Zondervan, 1983.

Lewis, Jack P. *The English Bible from the KJV to NIV: A History and Evaluation,* Second Ed. Baker, 1991.

McGrath, Alister. *In the Beginning: The Story of the King James Bible and How It Changed a Nation, a Language, and a Culture.* Anchor Books, 2001.

Metzger, Bruce M., Robert C. Dentan, Walter Harrelson. *The Making of the New Revised Standard Version of the Bible*. Eerdmans, 1991.

_____. *The Bible in Translation: Ancient and English Versions*. Baker Academic, 2001.

Nicolson, Adam. *God's Secretaries: The Making of the King James Bible*. HarperCollins Publishers, 2003.

Nida, Eugene A. and Charles R. Taber. *The Theory and Practice of Translation*. E.J. Brill, 1974.

Poythress, Vern S. and Wayne A. Grudem. *The TNIV and the Gender-Neutral Bible Controversy*. Broadman & Holman Publishers, 2004.

Porter, Stanley E. and Mark J. Boda, eds. *Translating the New Testament: Text, Translation, Theology*. Eerdmans, 2009.

Ryken, Leland. *The Word of God in English: Criteria for Excellence in Bible Translation*. Crossway Books, 2002.

_____. *Understanding English Bible Translation: The Case for an Essentially Literal Approach*. Crossway Books, 2009.

_____. *The Legacy of the King James Bible: Celebrating 400 Years of the Most Influential English Translation*. Crossway, 2011.

Scorgie, Galen G., Mark L. Strauss, and Steven M. Voth, eds. TH Challenge of Bible Translation. Zondervan, 2003.

Sheeley, Steven M. and Robert N. Nash, Jr. *The Bible in English Translation: An Essential Guide*. Abingdon Press, 1997.

Strauss, Mark L. *Distorting Scripture? The Challenge of Bible Translation & Gender Accuracy*. Intervarsity Press, 1998.

_____. "A Review of the Christian Standard Bible." *Themelios*, Vol.44, Issue 2, August 2019.

_____. "Why the English Standard Version (ESV) Should Not Become the Standard English Version." https://marklstrauss.com/articles.

Thomas, Robert L. *How to Choose a Bible Version: Making Sense of the Proliferation of Bible Translations.* Christian Forces Publications, 2000.

Waard, Jan de and Eugene A. Nida. *From One Language to Another: Functional Equivalence in Bible Translating*. Thomas Nelson, 1986.

Wallace, Foy E., Jr. *A Review of the New Versions*. Foy E. Wallace Jr. Publications, 1973.

Notes

Notes

Made in the USA
Columbia, SC
02 September 2024

41446497R00065